Safety, Security and Loss Prevention Management

Safety, Security and Loss Prevention Management

J.M. DIWAN

COMMONWEALTH PUBLISHERS

Safety, Security and Loss Prevention Management

Ist Edition : 1998
ISBN 81-7169-523-X

Published by :
Ajay Verma
for **Commonwealth Publishers**
4831/24, Prahlad Street,
Ansari Road, Darya Ganj,
New Delhi - 110002
Phone : 3272541, 3257835
Fax : 91-11-3257835

Laser Typesetting by :
Stylish Laser Typesetter,
Delhi.

Printed at :
Roshan Offset Printers,
Delhi-53. Ph. : 2260931

Preface

A company safety, security and loss prevention cannot be fully offensive if there is only partial participation by employees and management. The professional who expects to sell safety, security and loss prevention to management must get management involved in a total programme. The emphasis must be on preventing office accidents as well as production accidents. A key element on every successful organisation, in any successful accident prevention programme and in any occupation safety, security and loss prevention programme is effective job orientation and safety training. Workers must have proper training to do their jobs safely and efficiently.

The subject matter encompasses top, middle, and lower management. Special emphasis was placed on managing people, time, space, budgets, and resources to give the handbook extra utility for middle and lower management. Students of management in university or educational institutions will find the series an invaluable resource for adding "real world" practices to their academic and theoretical foundations. MBA students will gain an invaluable overview of the total organization to complement their MBA degree. Administrators and public managers can become acquainted with practices employed by managers and supervisors in private organizations. These practices are not always directly applicable in public sector bodies, but with thought and modifications, these private practices can adapt to public organizations. Public and university librarians will find the book an indispensable reference for the multitude of questions on many topics from the general public, special groups, associations, and students.

Editor

Contents

	Preface	v
1.	Office Safety	1
2.	Safety Training	32
3.	Safety Responsibilities	54
4.	Safety Administration	77
5.	Employee Attitude Towards Safety	86
6.	Effective Safety Programme	99
7.	Occupational Safety	105
8.	Mechanical Safety	122
9.	Industrial Safety	132
10.	Staffing and Controlling	159
11.	Organizing	198
12.	The Scope of Security and Loss Prevention	218
13.	Planning and Budgeting	239
	Index	273

1

Office Safety

Many large organisations today, such as insurance, governmental, and financial companies, consist almost entirely of office workers. Accidental injuries are just as painful, severe, and expensive when they occur to office workers as when they happen to production workers. Unless an organisation develops an effective office safety program, accidental injuries are far more likely to occur.

It is true that the risk of an occupation-related accident or injury to the office worker is lower than the risk to those employees involved in manufacturing or transportation. However, office risks often go unrecognised and unmanaged, and some could eventually lead to serious injuries and property loss.

A company safety program cannot be fully effective if there is only partial participation by employees and management. A safety program that is not vigorously pursued in company offices probably will not be vigorously pursued in the factory, shop, or plant. If office workers are exempt from safety policy, then production workers often feel that following rules to avoid hazards is an unnecessary burden, and, perhaps. An unfair exercise of authority by management. Exempt office workers seldom understand the importance of safety and may scoff at or criticise production-oriented safety activities, especially in front of production employees.

The health and safety professional who expects to

sell safety to management must get management involved in a total safety program. The emphasis must be on preventing office accidents as well as production accidents.

Seriousness of office injuries

One reason office safety programs are not more widespread is that many people believe office injuries are minor. This is a serious mistake. One aerospace firm, for example, paid out $102,000 over eight years at one facility just for injuries incurred by people falling out of chairs. Approximately 25,000 people worked at the plant, and more than half were office workers. Of the 14 chair accidents that occurred, the two worst cost the company a total of $97,000. Not only are medical and wage replacement benefits expensive for disabling accidents, but there also are hidden costs such as the loss of productivity.

Studies made by the State of California Department of Industrial relations and the Equitable Life Assurance Society of the United States show that this is not an isolated incident. The California Stat Department of Industrial Relations analysed reports filed by more than 3,000 California employers on disabling injuries to employees. These employers together employed more than one million office workers. "Office worker" was defined in the California study as "a person primarily engaged in performing clerical, administrative, or professional tasks indoors in an office at the employer's place of business." This definition did not cover salespersons, claims adjusters, social workers, medical and teaching personnel, and certain stock, order, and inventory clerks.

When the results of the study were extrapolated nationwide, investigators found that on-the-job office accidents amounted each year to about 40,000 disabling injuries at a direct cost of about $100 million. This figure does not include any indirect costs for employers, workers, or the nation.

Of the many accidental fatalities occurring to office workers, approximately half are work-connected automobile accidents. However, this amount can be significantly reduced by using a defensive driving program (DDC) such as that developed by the National Safety Council.

The California study did not cover employees of the federal government, maritime workers, and railroad workers in interstate commerce. The Equitable Life Assurance Society study, on the other hand, did include salespeople, claims adjusters, medical personnel, and supply and warehouse personnel. The insurance company study covered approximately 8,000 employees of one company working in one building, about 5% of whom were maintenance personnel. During the eight-year study period, the injury frequency rate was 2.3 and severity rate was 15 for the office workers.

Complacency—primary cause of injury

Complacency—the attitude that office accidents do not amount to much-is one of the prime causes of office accidents. The average office worker gives little thought to safety because office work is not perceived as being hazardous. Office injuries may seem to be inconsequential because they often lack dramatic impact. For example, the person who is injured falling backward from a chair seems to merit little sympathy or attention. The image of an office worker slipping and crashing to the floor on his back may even seem amusing to some people.

Industrial accidents are commonly considered to occur more frequently and with greater severity-

amputations, lost eyes, and broken bones-than office accidents. But who is likely to be absent from work longer: the office worker who sustains a severe compression fracture of one or more lumber vertebrae from a bad fall, or the production worker whose hand is amputated? Probably, it would be the office worker.

On the other hand, the well-instructed worker in a plant manufacturing flammable, toxic chemicals knows that it is a risky business-and understands why safe procedures must be used and safety equipment worn. The worker's safety behavior and training are the best defense. As a result, the production department may have fewer accidents than the plant office.

The office worker, therefore, has to be informed of the hazards and safe work procedures that apply to office jobs.

The employee must also be shown that management provides a safe environment and safe equipment to encourage proper safety behavior. The worker must be willing to adopt safe procedures, and be encouraged to do so. Even more important, office supervisors must understand the nature of office hazards and unsafe practices and take necessary measures to reduce and manage thee hazards.

The California and the Equitable Life studies pointed to whom most injuries occurred, and how they occurred.

New surroundings. These studies showed the importance of teaching office employees when working in new surroundings to look for new hazards and to correct them Studies revealed a substantial increase in the number of injuries in the first year a company moved into a new office building. The change upset established routines and presented unknown hazards. Even going to and from or became more hazardous as employees had to explore new driving and transportation routes.

New or young employees. The California study found that the new or younger employee does not have a higher accident rate than the longer employed and older worker-at least this was true for those employed in California. In California, office employees who had been on the job for one and two months has an injury percentage rate of 2.0% and 3.9% respectively. At the same time, those who had been employed for three to five years had the highest accident percentage rate (17.2%). As for age, the study showed that only 3% of the injuries occurred in the 18-to 10-years bracket.

Sex of employee. In the California study, 70% of the disabling injuries occurred to women, who comprised 68% of the office labour force. The study also shows that for office occupations, the estimated disabling work injury rate for women was very close to the injury rate for men. The rate as approximately 7.8 disabling injuries per 1,000 women employed in office work compared with 7.1 for the same number of men.

The injury statistics compiled from the California study were similar to the Equitable study. The rate of injury accidents per thousand male employees was about the same as it was for female employees. However, the rate of total days lost from disabling injuries was two and one-half to three times higher for men than for women.

Type of disabling accidents

Falls are the most common office accident and account for the most disabling injuries, according to both surveys. They cause from two to two and one-half times as high a disabling injury rate among office as among nonoffice employees. Falls were the most severe office accident and were responsible for 55% of the total days lost because of injuries.

Most chair falls came when a person was sitting down, rising, or moving about on a chair. A few were caused by people leaning back and tilting their chairs in the office or cafeteria, or putting their feet up on the desk. Although stairs seem more hazardous than chairs, people seem to recognise the stair hazard and are more cautious. Further more people are not as often exposed to the stair hazard as they are to a chair.

Another major accident category is falls on the same level. This includes slipping on wet or slippery and tripping over equipment, cords, or litter left on the floor. Good house-keeping procedures can reduce accidents in this category

A final category was falls from elevations, caused by standing on chairs or other office furniture and by falls from ladders, loading docks, or other miscellaneous elevations, These falls accounted for approximately 2% of the disabling injuries in the California study, whereas falls on stairs accounted for almost 5%.

Overexertion. Almost three-fourths of the strain or exertion mishaps occurred while employees were trying to move object-carrying or otherwise moving office machines, supplies, file drawers and trays, office furniture, heavy books, or other loads. Often , the employees were moving office equipment or furniture without authorisation from their supervisors. A significant number resulted when the employee made a sudden or awkward movement and did not involve any outside agency. Reaching, stretching, twisting, bending down, straightening up, and cumulative trauma were often associated with these injuries.

Objects striking or struck by workers. Objects striking office workers accounted for about 11% of the injuries in both studies, most of these injuries were sustained when the employee was struck by a falling object-file cabinets that became overbalanced when two or more drawers were open at the same time, file drawers that fell out when pulled too far, office machines and other objects that employees dropped on their feet when attempting a move, or typewriters that fell from a folding pedestal or rolling stand. In addition, a number of employees were struck by doors being opened from the other side. office supplies or other material and equipment sliding from shelves or cabinet tops caused a few injuries in this classification.

Striking against objects caused approximately 7% of the office injuries in both studies discussed here. Two out of three of these injuries were the result of bumping into doors, desks, file cabinets, open drawers, and even other people while walking. hitting open desk drawers or the desk itself, while seated at a desk, or striking open file drawers whole bending down or straightening up caused most of the rest of these injuries. Other incidents included workers bumping against sharp objects such as office machines, spindle files, staples, and pins. This category also comprised infected cuts incurred when employees handled paper, file drawers, and supplies.

Caught in or between. The final major classification was accidents where the worker was caught in or between machinery or equipment. Mostly, this was getting caught in a drawer, door, or window. However, a number of employees got caught in duplicating machines, copying machines, addressing machines, and fans, Several got their fingers under the knife edge of a cutter. Miscellaneous office accidents included foreign substances in the eye, spilled hot coffee or other hot liquid, burns from fire, insect bites, electric shocks, and paper cuts. Eyestrain or muscle aches from extended CRT/VDT use and cumulative trauma injuries also are to be considered hazards to office workers.

Controlling office hazards

Office accidents can be controlled by eliminating hazards or reducing exposure to them. Management can eliminate or reduce hazards most easily when the office is in the planning stage, when equipment is purchased, or when new office procedures are set up.

Layout and ambience

Office should be laid out for efficiency, convenience, and safety. The principles of workflow apply to offices as well as to factories. Location of the office should take into account the inherent hazards of adjoining operations.

Stairways and exits (including access and discharge) should comply with NFPA 101, Life Safety Code; floor and wall openings should comply with ANSI Construction Safety Requirements for Temporary Floor and Wall Openings, Flat Roots, Stairs, Railings, and Toeboards, A10.18 Handrails, not less than 30in. or more than 34 in. (0.8 and 0.9m) above the upper surface of the tread, are specified for one side of stairs up to 44in. (1.1m) wide, and both sides for stairs wider than 44 in. For stairs wider than 88 in (2.2 m) add an intermediate (center) rail.

Exits should be checked frequently to be sure that stair ways are unobstructed and well illuminated. Exit hallways or paths should have emergency lighting. Exit doors, if locked, should not require the use of a key for operation form inside the building.

Doors are another frequent source of accidents in offices, Glass doors should have some conspicuous design, either painted or deal about 4 ft above the floor and centered on the door so that people will not walk into it. Safety glass complying with ANSI standard Z97.1 should be installed, particularly in doors, rather then plate glass. Sometimes local codes specify the type that must be installed.

Forested safety glass windows in doors provide vision to prevent accidents while preserving privacy. Solid doors present at the same time, and one person can be struck when the door opens. Employees should be warned of this hazard and instructed (1) to approach a solid door in the proper manner, that is, away from the path of the opening door; (2) to reach for the other side, the hand receives the force of the impact rather than the face; and (3) to open the door slowly, especially if the door opens outward.

Another hazard is the door that opens directly onto a passageway. If the door opens directly into the path of oncoming traffic, somebody might bump into the edge of the door. If doors that open onto hallways cannot be recessed, they should be protected with short-angled deflector rails or U-shaped guardrails that protrude about 18 in. (46 cm) into the passageway. As an alternative,the area they swing over can be marked as suggested in the following paragraph. Another procedure is to place storage lockers or benches along the wall near the door, which provides the safety of a recessed door.

Some offices having tile floors will paint white or yellow stripes or apply tape to mark traffic flows or to guide people away form a rapidly opening door. The floor in front of a swinging door also can be marked or painted as a warning or a warning sign could be posted. As a final precaution, it is good practice to have the door hinges on the upstream side of the traffic; that is, on the righthand side as one faces the door from the hallways.

Lighting. Adequate light, ventilation, and other employee service have an important influence on employee morale. Business growth often requires installing more desks and other equipment than originally planned. Overcrowding is undesirable both for appearance and the physiological effect on employees, especially if it overtaxes ventilation facilities. Smaller offices can be made to appear larger and less crowded if walls, woodwork, and furniture are the same color.

Some accidents can be attributed to poor lighting. However, many less-tangible factors associated with poor illumination are contributing causes of office accidents. Some of these are direct glare, reflected glare from the work, and harsh shadows, all of which hamper sight.

Excessive visual fatigue can be an accident-causing element. Accidents also can be prompted by delayed eye adaptation when moving from bright surroundings into dark areas and vice versa. Some accidents attributed to an individual's carelessness can actually be traced to difficulty in seeing.

Office design can facilitate good lighting. If offices depend primarily on daylight, for example, employees engaged in visual tasks should be located near windows. North light is preferred by drafters and artists. However, employees generally should not face windows, unshielded lamps, or other sources of glare. Indirect, shielded fluorescent lamps can produce high levels of illumination without glare. Furthermore, walls and other surfaces should conserve light while avoiding annoying reflections. Ceiling, walls, and floor act as secondary large-area light sources and, if finished with he recommended reflecting paints or wall coverings, will increase light and reduce shadows. Finally, modern office lighting must be designed to counteract potential stress and eye fatigue in CRT/VDT users.

As a uniform means of evaluation, a standard procedure, entitled "How to Make a Lighting Survey" has been developed in cooperation with the U.S. Public Health Service.

Ventilation. For large interior spaces, forced

ventilation is needed if the space is to be used as an office area. All mechanical ventilation and comfort conditioning systems require careful planning and installation by qualified specialists. Private offices installed around the outer walls of a large office space should not cut off light and ventilation to other employees. If fans are used in an office, they should be guarded, secured, and placed where they cannot fall.

The designs of many office buildings seal in office air-odors, smoke, office solvents and chemicals, molds, fungus, and other contaminants. In these buildings, it is particularly important to design and install adequate ventilation systems. Management should regularly inspect the systems and update them if problems appear.

Electrical. Management must protect workers against electrical equipment hazards in an office. In some cases, the hazard can be avoided completely, such as not using electric key switches. In other cases, hazards can be reduced by using UL-listed equipment, use of ground-fault circuit interrupters (GFCI), installing sufficient well-located outlets (receptacles),

Employee should not use poorly maintained, unsafe, or poor-quality, no-UL-listed electrical equipment, such as coffee makers, radios, and lamps. Such appliances can create fire and shock hazards.

The company should make sure that a sufficient number of outlets are installed to eliminate the need for extension cords. Those that are necessary should be clipped to backs of desks or taped down. If cords cannot be dropped from overhead and must cross the floor, cover them with rubber channels designed for this purpose. Cords should not rest on steam pipes or other hot or sharp metallic surfaces.

Outlets should accommodate three-wire grounded

plugs to help prevent electric shock to operators. Floor outlets should be located, if possible, so they are not tripping hazards and cannot be accidentally kicked or used as a foot rest. A floor outlet protruding above floor level is frequently shielded by a desk or some other piece of furniture. However, when the desk is moved, the outlet can become an immediate tripping hazard unless it is appropriately covered. Such floor design is not common any longer; underfloor or cellular floor raceways are usually used in new construction.

The national Electrical Code, ANSI/NFPA 70, requires GFCI in restroom areas. In all areas, wall receptacles should be so designed and installed that no current-carrying parts will be exposed, and outlet plates should be kept tight to eliminate possibility of shock or collision injury.

Cords for electrically operated office machines, fans, lamps, and other equipment should be properly installed and frequently inspected to see if there are any defects that can cause shocks or burns. Switches should be provided, either in the equipment or in the cords, so workers do not have to pull the plugs to shut off the power. The fact that office equipment is operated on 110-volt circuits is no assurance that serious injury will not occur.

Office electrical service should be designed to accommodate changes in equipment and technology. Electrical, coaxial, computer, and telephone cables are easily serviced and moved when run through modular channels dropped from the ceiling.

Installation or repair of any electrical equipment should be done by qualified workers using only approved materials. Because defective wiring may constitute both shock and fire hazards, management and workers must observe all recommendations of the National Electrical Code, ANSI/NFPA 70.

Equipment. Workers should never place an office machine on the edge of a table or desk. Maintenance staff or manufacturer representatives should secure machines that tend to creep during operation. they can either affix the machines directly to the desk or table or place them on a nonslip pad. In particular, typewriters on folding pedestals should be fastened to the pedestal.

Workers should place heavy equipment and files against walls or columns; files also can be place against railings. File cabinets should be bolted together or fastened to the floor or wall so workers cannot to them over.

Floors. Floor surfaces are one of the major causes of office accidents. They should be as durable and maintenance free as possible. Management should select floor finishes for slip-resistant qualities. Well-maintained carpet provides good protection against slips and falls. Maintenance staff must repair defective tiles, boards, or carpet immediately. They should also replace or repair worn or warped mats under office chairs and rubber or plastic floor mats with curled edges or tears. These conditions can create tripping hazards.

Highly polished and extremely hard but unwaxed surfaces such as marble, terrazzo, and steel plates represent slipping hazards. Slip-resistant floor wax can give these materials a higher coefficient of friction and can reduce their slipping hazard. However, maintenance staff must not apply wax so use an oil mop on a waxed floor because it creates a soft, smeary coating that could become a slipping hazard.

Special slip-resistant protection should be used on stairways and at lobby or elevator entrances. Be sure these especially hazardous areas are always maintained in the best possible condition. Floor mats and runners often provide a better, more slip-resistant waling surface.

Outdoor areas. Parking lots and sidewalks represent major problem areas. Many slipping and failing accidents occur in the company parking lot. To reduce the hazards, maintenance workers must keep the lot clear, remove debris, fill potholes, and correct uneven surfaces. In colder climates, effective snow and ice removal controls should be used during the winter months.

Aisles and stairs. A suggested minimum width for aisles if four feet. All aisles and passageways must meet the width requirements of NFPA 101, Life Safety Code. Keep passages through the work area unobstructed, and place wastebaskets where people will not trip over them. Be sure to install telephone cables and electrical outlets so their wires do not create a tripping hazard in passageways. These and other obstructions, such as low tables and office equipment, should be placed against walls or partitions, under desks or in corners. Avoid building stepoffs from one level to another in an office; if one exists it should be well marked and guarded with a railing.

File drawers should not open into aisles, particularly narrow ones, unless extra space is provided. Pencil sharpeners and typewriters carriages must not just out into aisles.

Storage. Materials stored in office sometimes cause problems. In general, materials should be stored in areas specifically set aside for the purpose. The storage area should be located so general traffic patterns do not have to be crossed to reach the stored items. Also, workers should not store or leave anything on the floor in a passageway where it could become a tripping hazard.

Train workers to stack materials in stable piles that will not fall over. They should put the heaviest and largest pieces on the bottom of the pile. When materials are stored on shelves, they heavy objects should be on the lower shelves. Workers should not stack objects on window sills if there is a danger the objects may break the window or fall through it.

Supervisors and managers should plan storage areas to make item easily accessible. Appropriate stepladders should be provide where necessary. Office falls can occur when workers stand on chairs, counters, or shelves to reach inconveniently stored items. Rolling ladders are discussed in the next section, Safe Office Equipment.

Companies should prohibit smoking in mailing, shipping print shops, or receiving rooms. They should also can smoking in other areas where large quantities of loose paper and other combustible material may be stored and in areas where flammable fluids are used, such as duplicating rooms or artists' supply areas.

Workers should store flammable and combustible fluids and similar materials in safety cans, preferably in locked and identified cabinets. Only minor quantities should be left in the office, and bulk storage should be in properly constructed fireproof vaults.

Safe office equipment

Good quality office furniture not only contributes to the safety of the office but also enhances its appearance. This, in turn, improves the attitudes of both employees and visitors.

Chairs, especially, should be comfortable and sturdily built with a wide enough base to prevent easy tipping. Five-legged chairs are more stable and discourage employees from tilting back on their chairs. The casters on swivel chairs should be on at least a 20-in

(0.5 m) diameter base, but a 22-in. base is preferred. the casters should be securely fixed to the base of the chair and well constructed because loose or broken casters are a frequent cause of chair falls. About 20% of the chair falls in the California study were due to chair defects.

Companies should purchase chairs with easy-to-adjust sear heights and back supports. Show employees how to properly adjust their chairs. The correct fit will make the employee more comfortable and help to reduce acute and chronic back strain-enabling office workers to work more safely and productively.

Desks and files. Spring-loaded typing desks should be carefully selected. If a worker opens some models without due care, the typewriter table will snap out and could bruise or cut the person.

Also, even if good quality desks and file cabinets are purchased, it is still possible that occasionally one will have a sharp burr or corner on it. Supervisors or maintenance staff should inspect office furniture when it is received and remove such burrs or corners immediately. Drawers on desks and file cabinets should have safety stops to prevent workers from pulling them out of the drawer slot.

Other safety tips can help to prevent accidents and injuries. purchase office machines, such as rotary files, copying machines, paper cutters, and paper shredders, with well-designed guards. Glass tops on desks and tables can crack and cause safety hazards. Durable synthetic surfaces are safer. Make sure workers have enough noncombustible wastebaskets. If smoking is permitted in the area, provide safety-type ashtrays that are large and stable enough to safely contain smoking materials.

Office fans should have substantial bases and

convenient attachments for moving and carrying. If located less than 7 ft. (2.1 m) form the floor, they must be well guarded, front and back, with mesh to prevent workers' fingers from getting inside the guard. Many cut fingers result when people try to move fans by grasping the guard or try to catch falling fans. Train workers not to handle fans until they shut off the power and the blades stop turning.

Computers. If a computer is to be installed in a building with overhead sprinklers, keep sprinkler protection in service throughout the area, but get advice on necessary protection against both fire and water damage to computer hardware. Actually, water damage is not to be feared as much as previously thought. For one thing, most new computers are less susceptible because of their solid-state circuitry. In addition, tests have shown that water does not harm magnetic tape. Most of the damage suffered by computers in a fire results from the hear. One of the best ways to prevent a damaging fire is to keep combustible materials such as paper, tapes, and cards at an absolute minimum in the room with the computer. When safeguarding such an investment, call in a fire protection adviser as well as a computer installation expert.

Rolling ladders and stands used for reaching high storage should have brakes that operate automatically when weight is applied to them. All stepladders should have nonskid feet.

Chemical products. Organisations often underestimate the number and types of hazards represented by office chemicals. The safety professional should assess all chemical products used in copying and duplicating machines and in print shops and should assess all adhesives and cleaning materials. Workers must be informed of any dangers and instructed in the safe use of hazardous chemical products.

If possible, substitute nontoxic and nonflammable solvents for those used in printing and duplicating or other operations. If chlorinated bleaches are purchased for cleaning purposes, make sure that they will not be mixed with strongly acidic or easily oxidized materials. Purchase a good grade of slip-resistant floor wax.

Purchasing equipment. The company health and safety professional should work with the purchasing agent in buying office furniture and equipment. Both should be aware that although advertisers sometimes stress the safety features of office equipment, the machines may be delivered without these important safeguards. Mechanical hazards of heavy office equipment can be determined by careful expert inspection before purchase. These hazards can almost always be eliminated or minimised, although sometimes at substantial expense.

The safety professional should also inform the purchasing department of precautions to be taken in connection with chemicals, dyes, inks, and other supply irritant, or flammable properties. Where hazards are unavoidable, manufacturers, suppliers, or the safety department should supply labels and specific instructions for careful handling or issue instructions when workers receive the material.

The purchasing should gather all pertinent information form the manufacturer on equipment design and electrical and space requirements, and should try to determine the composition of proprietary compounds. They can forward this information to the safety professional (or safety department) for an opinion concerning inherent safety hazards before purchasing new equipment or supplies

Office machines. All machines having external moving parts that could be hazardous should have enforced safety procedures and constant training and retraining of operators as necessary. Tell employees that if any office machine gives a shock, appears defective, sparks, or smokes, they should turn it off, pull the plug, and inform the supervisor.

Some office machines are noisy, especially the telex, computer printers, and printing equipment. This noise is usually more of an annoyance than a health hazard, but may need to be evaluated by a professional for possible adverse effects. Various covers help to dampen machine noise.

Printing services

Larger offset presses. Check the operation of offset presses. Is the operator putting his or her fingers on the blanket while the press is in motion? One offset press department had seven finger-injury accidents in the first two weeks of operation, all caused by press operators who put their fingers in the running press to remove dirt or other particles from the plate. Presses should meet all guarding regulations imposed by local, state or provincial, and federal agencies.

Make sure the area around the presses is free form clutter and well lighted. The flooring should be resilient, or rubber mats should be provided to minimise operator fatigue and to prevent slipping.

Only qualified operators should operate presses. Loose clothing and long hair are hazardous around these machines. Train workers to use a safe, nontoxic substance to clean the press; office supervisors and press operators should understand the fire and possible health hazards involved and follow all instructions for safe use and storage. The disposal of cleaning materials should be planned so that the procedure is an acceptable practice.

Gathering and stitching machines. Supervisors should make sure guards are installed on open sprockets and collector chain drives of gathering and wire stitching (or stapling) machines to protect employees from hand and body injury. The operating arm on the end of the gathering machine should be guarded.

Install hinged drop-guards to cover any exposed operating mechanism that creates nipping hazards under the machine and along the working area where operators fill the pockets. Nonskid material should cover the floors and work platform at this area. Supervisors should train operators to open signatures in the middle and place them on the saddle or rod between the hooks on the moving chain. If the hook is not put on the rod or chain correctly, workers must shut off the machine before attempting to straighten the hook out. Operators should also shut down the machine when threading stitcher heads, making any adjustments, or removing jams.

Folding machines. Here are points to be stressed for safe operation of folding machines:

1. Before jammed paper is pulled from the machine, shut the motor off to avoid getting hands in the feed rollers.
2 Finger clearance at the folding knife should be checked before pulling out paper, putting tape on rollers, or adjusting plates and roller pressure.
3 Workers should walk down the steps of folder feeder platforms facing forward, never backward.
4 On large-sized folders, all steps and platforms should be protected by railings.

Defective staples protruding from reports or booklets should be removed to avoid cuts from them while books are being jogged, trimmed, or wrapped. Workers should be trained to cup their hands over the work when removing defective wire staples. Employees engaged in this operation should wear eye or face protection, and passers-by should be protected against flying staples by screens or by isolation of this work.

Enforced safety procedures

Because the major category of office accidents is slops and falls, employees should never run in office. Also, a number of office accidents can be prevented if everyone walking in passageways would keep to the right. Convex mirrors should be placed—and used—at corners and other blind intersections. Collisions at doors also can be prevented if people do not stand directly at doors also can be prevented if people do not stand directly in front of the door, but away the path of its swing when they go to open it.

People carrying material must be sure they can see over and around it when walking though the office. They should not carry stacks of materials on stairs but use the elevator instead. If one is not available, the person should make two trips. People should not have both arms loaded when using stairs; one hand should be free to use the handrail.

When using stairs outside at night or in a dimly lit area, workers should be instructed to go single file, to keep to the crowd or push on stairways; they should pay attention to where they are going. Falls on stairs often occur when the person is talking, laughing, and turning to friends while going downstairs. Other safety rules for stairs include: don not congregate on stairs or landings, and do not stand near doors at the head or foot of stairways.

Good housekeeping is essential to prevent falls. Employees should not be permitted to litter in their work areas and should wide up all spilled liquids immediately. Pieces of paper clips, rubber bands, pencils, and other loose objects must be picked up as soon as they are spotted.

Whoever breaks any glass should sweep it up at once. Do not allow employees to discard loose broken glass in a waste container. Instead, tell them to wrap it in heavy paper and mark it Broken Glass for Disposal. Glass that shatters into fine pieces can be picked up with damp paper towels.

All tripping hazards, such as defective floors, rugs, or floor mats, should be reported to the maintenance department and immediately repaired. Many falls could be prevented if employees wore supportive footwear with nonslip soles; shoes with high heels are undesirable.

Chair falls. Habits that lead to chair falls must be discouraged. Supervisors should instruct employees not to scoot across the floor while sitting on a chair not to lean sideways from the chair to pick up objects on the floor. Discourage workers from leaning back in the chair and placing their feet on the desk. It is easy to fall over backwards in this position.

People should properly seat themselves in their chairs.They should form the habit of placing a hand behind them to make sure the chair is in place, Sitting down on the edge of the seat rather than in the center, or backing too far without looking, or kicking the chair out from under can result in sudden fall to the floor. standing on a chair to reach an overhead object is particularly dangerous and must be forbidden.

Filing cabinets, are a major cause of injuries. These include bumped heads from getting up too quickly under open drawers, mashed fingers form improperly closing drawers, and hand injuries and strains from moving the cabinets.

Some precautions are necessary against these accidents:

- People should never close file drawers with their feet or any other part of their body. They should use the drawer handle to close the cabinet, making sure their fingers are not curled over the edge when the drawer closes. All file drawers should be closed immediately after use.
- Employees should open only one file drawer in the cabinet at a time to prevent the cabinet from toppling over. As previously indicated, where possible, have the file cabinets bolted together or otherwise secured to a stationary object to safeguard against this chance of human failure
- Do not open a file drawer if someone is close by or underneath and could be injured by the drawer. Do not leave an open drawer unattended-not even for a minute. Whoever opens a file drawer should warm others working in the area so they do not turn around or straighten up quickly and bump or trip over an open drawer. Workers should never climb on open drawer
- Small stools used in filing areas are tripping hazards when lift in passageways. Any person who sees one out of place should put it where it cannot cause a fall.
- Filing personnel should wear rubber finger guards to eliminate cut fingers from metal fasteners or paper edges.

Office personnel should never move desks or files; they should be moved by maintenance workers preferably using special dollies or trucks, In general, furniture should not be rearranged without authorisation from office management. When desks or cabinets are moved, workers should consider whether they will obstruct floor space or aisles before making the move. If a telephone terminal box on the floor or electrical outlet box is exposed after moving furniture, the box should be marked with a tripping hazard sign until it is removed. Maintenance staff must remove the outlet and, if it is needed, relocate it; this step is far cheaper than to pay for a fall. Do not run electric cords under rugs; they sometimes come out because of traffic movement and form tripping hazards. They also are fire hazards. New outlets should be installed to climate the necessity for extension cords.

Materials storage. There are a number of precautions to be taken when storing materials. Neat storage makes it easier to find and recover materials without dropping or knocking over other materials. Supervisors must keep employees from stacking boxes, papers, and other heavy objects on file cabinets, desks, and window ledges, of from placing these materials carelessly on shelves where they could tumble down in an avalanche. If heavy objects fall toward a window, the glass might break and cause a serious accident.

Instruct workers not to place card index files, dictionaries, or other heavy objects on top of file cabinets and other high furniture. Movable objects such as flowerpots, vases, and bottles should not be allowed on windowsills or ledges. Caution workers not to throw loose razor blades, thumbtacks, and other sharp objects into their drawers but to put them in small boxes. Tools with blades and points should have the cutting or sharp end stuck in foamed-polystyrene blocks.

Lifting. Occasionally it is necessary for office personnel to lift light or heavy objects, such as files, books, boxes, and computer tapes. For these times, make sure office workers are trained in proper lifting techniques.

Other hazards. some additional hazards are all follows: (1) never allow a spindle (spike) file in the office; (2) never store pencils in a glass on the desk with points outward; (3) never leave a knife or scissors on a desk with the point toward the user and never hand sharp-pointed objects to anyone, point first; (4) equip paper cutters with a guard that affords maximum protection (bar guards or single-rod barriers found in some cutters are not considered full protection); and (5) do not leave glass objects on the edge of desks or tables where they can easily be pushed off. Make sure that office machinery is operated only by authorised persons.

Some offices have an employee lounge or eating area with a hot plate for brewing coffee or a microwave over for warming lunches. In these areas, spilled beverages can be a burning and a slipping hazard. Microwave ovens must be properly used to avoid injuries or damage to the oven.

If the sales departmt nt is part of the office staff, or if employees travel on company business, a safe program. Supervisors should encourage employees to report all broken chairs, missing casters, stuck drawers, cracked glass, and other hazards for correction. Management should establish a policy for immediate correction of these defects and set up a formal program requiring quarterly office safety inspections.

File protection

Fire hazards. To prevent spontaneous combustion fires, store all solvent-soaked or oily rags used for cleaning duplicating equipment in a metal safety container. Management should prohibit smoking within 10 ft (3 m) of where flammable solvents are used in duplicating or any other office operations. Workers should be trained in handling solvents to prevent eye injuries form splashes and wear proper protective equipment.

In recognition of the health hazards caused by smoking, many organisations do not allow smoking at any place in the facility. Other safety rules regarding smoking include (1) never allow smoking on elevators and (2) do not throw matches or cigarettes into wastebaskets; the contents usually are highly combustible. Supervisors or department heads should establish procedures so cleaning and maintenance personnel do not collect possible smoldering combustible material from ashtrays and throw it into combustible containers, such as cardboard boxes or cloth bags.

Some waste containers made from plastic or other flame-resistant material may actually be combustible if subjected to fire or intense heat. Such fires can generate dangerous toxic gases and dense smoke that can easily endanger a whole office. To control this hazard, use only metal or fire-safe tested materials designed to contain the fire.

Fire extinguishers. portable fire extinguishers in a fully charged, operable condition must be kept in their designated places at all times when they are not used.

Employees in general should know what to do in case of fire. Supervisors must train workers to operate extinguishers and fire hoses, if provided, and show them how to react in case of fire or other emergency. (Panic and confusion can be as dangerous as flame and smoke.)

When a fire is discovered, an employee should do three things: (1) turn in the alarm (no matter how small the fire is), (2) alert fellow workers, and (3) if trained to do so, use the proper firefighting equipment, but only if the employee always has a safe path of escape while fighting the fire.

Office employees should receive annual fire and other emergency training. The training should include use of portable fire extinguishers, procedures for reporting emergencies, and location of escape routes and shelters.

Emergency plan. Every office should have a written emergency plan, Supervisors should be appointed in every area to safely guide people out of the building. Every department should be assigned a specific route, and an alternate, in case the exist is blocked. A surprise fire drill may save lives in an emergency situation in the future.

When the alarm sounds, supervisors should direct the show, but every employee must play a part. The group should move calmly along in an businesslike manner, without hurrying or pushing, and wait on a different floor or outside the building for the signal to return. In a real emergency, the officials in charge would authorise return to the building,

Ergonomics in the office

Much care and consideration needs to be focused on the design of workstations and how equipment is used at the workstation. At the least, the supervisor or department head should be concerned with the selection of proper chairs, position of the individual in relation to the work surface, arrangement of work materials, and the proper use of video display terminals (VDT) at workstations.

A more in-depth ergonomic approach would include a survey of the office environment. Factors such as general lighting considerations, computer-terminal lighting, room temperature and drafts. ventilation, and noise would be included.

Safety organisation in the office

The supervisor is, of course, the key person in the office

safety program. However, even the hardest working supervisor will have difficulty maintaining full-time interest in safety all alone. on the other hand, the office safety committee can help to maintain interest in the accident prevention program, but it cannot substitute for good management.

Safety and health training

Safety training has a tendency to be overlooked in an office environment. All office workers should be provided with safety training that focuses on accident prevention, fire prevention, fire emergency response, and medical emergency response. Depending on the specific nature of the office environment, hazard communications training may be required. If an office environment contains an art department, print shop, or duplicating center, hazard communications training should be given to all employees.

To develop proper safety behavior, supervisors must provide safety instructions for all new office employees. The personnel or industrial relations department can supply an accident prevention brochure or a set of printed rules. They also should arrange for all explanations of procedures as quickly as possible during the employee's early workdays.

Unfamiliar surroundings, new equipment, or altered work tasks increase the likelihood of accidents, even among veteran employees. Therefore, these people also should be trained when beginning a new job and given specific instructions for each piece of equipment. No one should ever be permitted to use a machine unless fully instructed in its operation and shown the location of fire equipment, how to use it, and how to summon medical aid.

Supervisors should have instruction in safe office

operation because they are likely to be as unaware of accident hazards and the employees. However, prevention of accidents requires the dedicated vigilance of the supervisor throughout every working day. If he or she fails to carry out this function, the number of accidents due to unsafe practices by employees will continue undiminished.

Routine safety and health training should be part of company policy, and employees should receive continuing information on work-related hazards and safe practices. Training meetings are recommended on such topics as slip and fall prevention, proper lifting, fire safety, emergency procedures, office chemical safety and off-the-job safety. Safe attitudes and behavior are not merely put on when an employee enters the office and taken off when the individual walks out the front door.

All office employees who much enter production areas where safety hats, eye protection, and hearing protection are necessary must be provided with these items and shall be required to wear them. Every employee who visits the plant should have card of the general safety rules that apply to the plant and should be familiar with them. The same requirement should be enforced for all visitors. Safety rules should apply to everyone if the program is to be successful.

Another critical aspect of training focuses on ergonomic and stress-related areas. Supervisors need to educate workers to recognise common physical complaints that could be caused by the ergonomic design of the workstation or how they use equipment at the workstation. Common physical complaints include eyestrain; back pain; neck pain, shoulder and arm symptoms; wrist, hand and finger symptoms; leg and foot symptoms; headache; and fatigue. Training materials should emphasise how employees can change their work habits or adapt equipment and furniture to reduce these complaints.

Office workers tend to work under a high level of stress. One definition of stress is an employee's physical and emotional reaction to change. A definite focus of training should be stress reduction and occupational wellness. Workers can be stress physical symptoms of stress overload, and use various methods to alleviate stress. Stress reduction programs can include progressive relaxation, positive imagery, values clarification, proper nutrition, and exercise. Many other programs can be developed that focus on occupational wellness.

Finally, a company safety program cannot succeed unless it has the whole-hearted backing of its top management. Supervisors must know that their accident prevention performance is watched and that good performance is appreciated. The Council's Supervisors' Safety Manual contains information on this topic that can guide both top management and the safety professional.

Safety and health committee

In planning an office safety program, management should ensure that worker representation on the safety and health committee reflects the composition of the workforce in company departments or divisions.

The office should be on the inspection itinerary of the company's safety professional. The office supervisor should accompany safety inspector on every inspection, along with an office safety committee member. The committee's responsibilities include helping all supervisor maintain safe working conditions in office areas. The committee reports directly to the safety director or whoever is in charge of the programs. Along with the department head, it can make periodic inspections of the office to look for accident or fire hazards. The committee makes recommendations, many of them based on suggestions from supervisors and other employees. It is also can help to prepare and revise company safety rules.

Often the committee is in charge of office-wide communication, training, and incentive programs. These are designed to maintain peak interest in safety, and use such means as posters, bulletins, and contests.

Accident records

If a safety program is to succeed, the company needs to keep accurate accident records. Not only do accident investigations and analysis of records spotlight problems that must be corrected, but the records show if the company is making progress in accident prevention.

Office employees, like plant workers, should report every accident, no matter how minor the injury. The reports should be detailed and made as quickly as possible following the accident or near accident. Unsafe conditions or procedures indicated in the reports should be corrected as quickly as possible, because near-miss accidents are warnings of worse accidents to come.

Records are the concrete foundation of the safety structure. They tell the "who, what, when, why, and how" of accidents in the office-and help supervisors and employees to prevent repeat performances. Accurate records also provide guidelines on which company insurance rates are based.

The average office will not have enough major injuries to warrant extensive investigation and analysis. However, it is urgent that records be kept to pinpoint problems and prevent future accidents. If, for instance, a large number of falls are injuring workers, supervisors can double-check possible hazards and devote special attention to the problem in meetings and other communications. Standard report forms are available.

2

Safety Training

A key element on every successful orgnisation, in any successful accident prevention program, and in any occupational safety and health program is effective job orientation and safety training. Workers must have proper training to do their jobs safely and efficiently.

The responsibility for, and the implementation of, employee training rests with management. Management must recognise that for the orgnisation to achieve its objective employees need to perform at a certain level. In order to achieve a satisfactory level of achievement, management needs to establish worker training policies. This in turn will lead to programs for the workers. To help achieve this goal, line managers must:

1. understand how to train employees in the safest and most efficient methods of job performance
2. know and support all company health and safety policies and procedures
3. know how to detect and eliminate or control hazards, investigate accidents, and handle emergency situations
4. be trained in the proper methods of leadership and supervision.

Safety and health professionals should be taught how to identify and employ sound training methods. In the event the company hires training consultants, the safety orgnisation must ensure that the instruction they provide achieves the company's goals and meets all regulatory training obligations.

Training as part of the safety program

A new era in worker safety and health has arrived in the past two decades, and the need for training is being addressed by regulatory and legislative bodies. The responsibility for safety training typically falls under the jurisdiction of the safety and health professional. Whether members of the safety department actually conduct the classes or merely ensure they are conducted depends on the individual orgnisation. Orgnisations can longer simply provide a training session, however; the emphasis must be on workers demonstrating satisfactory understanding of how to perform various work procedures using safety equipment, proper guarding, and proper maintenance. With this in mind, it is critical for the safety and health professional to work closely with all levels of management and employees to ensure that raining is adequate, accurate, and timely.

Management from top executives to supervisors must recognise the importance of training and support training efforts if these programs are to have is not important to their supervisors, it will not be important to them.

There are several ways for the safety and health professional to identify the training needs of the orgnisation. The professional can work with company legal counsel and others to stay current with all regulations mandating specific safety requirements. Accident and injury records together with specific investigation reports can reveal areas of weakness or failure in training. Although this approach looks at the past, it can turned into a proactive approach designed to prevent similar incidents from occurring. According to

Heinrich's theory, past events forecast the possibility of future and potentially more severe incidents.

Other ways the safety and health professional can determine training needs include workplace surveys, regularly scheduled inspections, and employee opinion surveys. These are preventive methods used to identify training needs so that programs can be established before more accidents occur.

Safety and health professionals must keep in mind that training programs do not eliminate a company's obligation to provide safe working conditions or to remove unsafe materials from the workplace. Training, however, will ensure that employees know how to do their jobs using the proper methods. Reports have strongly suggested that the majority of accidents are caused by workers' unsafe practices and errors rather than by equipment failures or poor engineering. At least in part, training can change undesired behavior and/or reinforce the desired behavior.

Training, unfortunately, is not the answer to all work-related problems. It is only one method of influencing human behavior. Before a training program is developed, management should thoroughly evaluate all problems and expectations related to the operation to determine if training will accomplish the desired goals. It must be clearly understood by everyone that training can be used only to correct skill deficiencies or to improve knowledge. Most training programs cannot correct poor engineering, poor worker attitudes, or substitute for good safety engineering and enforcement.

Training policy

In many orgnisations, written policy statements establish the purpose, goals, and procedures for such areas as the company mission, hiring practices, purchasing, and so on. A written statement should be developed to cover the orgnisation's policy on training. This may be incorporated into an overall policy statement or into separate policies for each issue.

Whichever method management selects, it should keep certain considerations in mind. The first concern is that all policies must be written to work together to achieve the ultimate company objective. Too often policies are developed separately and tend to conflict with one another. When this occurs, supervisors and workers become confused and may show inconsistent compliance. Thus, management must make sure that when several policy statements are used, they do not contradict one another.

A second consideration is the development of training schedules for all employees. A common error, found in many orgnisations, is to focus on safety training for workers and possibly supervisors and neglect to provide supportive training for management. This oversight can develop into a conflict of interest" situation because the management team is unaware of the activities of the safety program. When managers understand the orgnisation's safety efforts, they find it easier to support them.

Therefore, the orgnisation's training policy should define training programs for all levels of management and employees. The importance of this policy cannot be underestimated. Many of the difficulties companies experience in trying to provide safety training are a result of communication problems between different levels of the management team. Likewise, many of these same problems could be resolved by training managers in such areas as their legal obligations, their safety mission, savings potential of safety training, and other concerns.

A strong training policy will avoid pitting the safety orgnisation against management over training issues. The policy should identify the type of training to be provided for workers, line supervisors, and management personnel. Elements of the program, such as the type of training methods used and the location of the training, may also be specified.

A well-planned training program should never interfere with production schedules. The policy statement can help to reinforce the principle that safety training is good business and can actually improve production rather than interfere with it as some managers may believe.

Planning the training program in advance will help to prevent any friction that may otherwise occur between departments. When management staff is guided by a policy statement, the training program becomes part of the company's overall operational standards and will be incorporated into the schedule rather than regarded as an interruption.

Training budgets

To establish an effective safety training program, management must provide an adequate budget. Training is an area where the old adage "you get what you pay for" is decidedly true. The budget for safety training may either be included with other training may either be included with other training programs to be divided into separate accounts, depending on the company's financial policies.

When safety training is combined with other training programs, workers more easily accept the message that safety is a part of day-to-day operations. On the other hand, if safety training is separate from, say job skill training, employees and managers may rend to regard safety as less important.

The costs of training must be accurately recorded. These costs include but are not limited to:

- physical space
- personnel staffing
- student salaries
- training materials
- downtime
- personnel replacements
- transportation costs
- lodging, meals, etc.

Each orgnisation has its own financial accounting practices. The important element in evaluating program costs is to be sure to identify the complete costs of any training program. Even though many of these expenses are only indirectly related, they are still a legitimate part of the program budget.

The decision to train workers in safety is made by comparing the costs of undertaking such training against the costs of no training at all. The cost of not training must also reflect all of the possible expenses associated with worker accidents and injuries. For example, a training program for teaching proper lifting procedures may be estimated at $25,000. However, not training workers in these procedures may result in injuries that can amount to annual costs several times higher than the $25,000 estimated for the safety programs. Thus, the company could easily recoup the cost of training by preventing even one injury to only one employee. These figures are only examples. But by reviewing recorded, the safety and health professional can identify thc average cost of a particular class of injury and the number of these injuries experienced annually and compare this figure to the cost of providing a safety training program that will correct the problem.

With the support of the training policy, it is possible to prepare adequate budgets to provide all elements of a strong safety training program. These elements include:

1. planning company training need before an accident or series of accidents
2. considering company growth or expansion
3. meeting all regulatory requirements
4. evaluating past accident causes
5. eliminating or controlling known hazards
6. providing adequate recordkeeping
7. providing for personnel development trainers supervisors, etc)

Recordkeeping

Along with the increased emphasis on employee training by regulatory agencies, there has been a corresponding emphasis on company recordkeeping. Besides using records to fulfill legal obligations, orgnisations are also finding valuable used for training records within their orgnisations. For example, an orgnisation may need to demonstrate the comprehensive nature of its training program should a worker or manager file a lawsuit as the result of an accident or injury. Training records will help to identify the strengths and weaknesses of the safety program. In addition, future training budgets can be developed by examining the effectiveness and costs of past training programs.

Both new and current employees require regular safety training. In order to ensure that every member of the orgnisation has received the appropriate training and is scheduled to receive additional instruction when required, the company must maintain adequate records for each employee. If a worker is injured, his or her records may provide valuable information to identify the true cause of the accident. Training records should also document who were the instructors for the training session, the cost of each training session, the content and methods used for instruction, and the results or effectiveness of each training session.

Employees' personal training records should be securely maintained to ensure privacy yet still permit employees to see their files. Accident investigators and regulatory representative may also need to have access to these records for reasons.

Standards employee records include:

- employee work history
- job descriptions and locations of work performed
- specific task performance training programs attended
- dates and costs of training.
- location of training session
- purpose of training.

Additional information in the records can include:

- course title
- course objectives
- training methods
- training aids or course materials used
- instructor
- methods of evaluation.

The company must have a written policy identifying who

is allowed access to the training records and under what conditions. This policy should be developed under the guidance of legal counsel.

Safety training needs

A safety training program is needed under the following conditions:

1. for all new or reassigned employees
2. when new equipment or processes are introduced
3. whenever procedures are revised or updated
4. when new information is available or required
5. when employee performance needs improvement or to provide employee growth

6 when employee interest in safety and efficiency needs a boost.

Many orgnisations mistakenly assume that transferred employees will not require orientation to their new assignments because they already know the operations. This assumption has been responsible for many worker injuries. In many instances, a transferring worker requires almost the same type of orientation as does a newly hired employee. Information should be presented on the location of safety equipment. Material Safety Data Sheets, MSDS files, proper accident and first aid reporting procedures, evacuation procedures, and other items differ form workstation to workstation. For transferred employees to work safety and efficiently, management must orient them to the new environment.

Certain symptoms will indicate to the alert safety and health professional that training is needed. These symptoms include:

1. proportionately higher accidents of injury rates than other companies that do the same type of work.

2. increasing accidents rates and/or insurance rates
3. high employee turnover
4. excessive waste and/or scrap materials from operations
5. recent company expansion or procedural changes
6. increased or high levels of sick days
7. changing regulatory requirement
8. need to upgrade or update employees; knowledge and/or responsibilities
9. poor job satisfaction.

Orgnisations that have had great success in developing safe working environments understand the importance of the supervisor's role. Therefore, they focus considerable safety training on first-line supervisors. This does not eliminate the need to train all managers and employees but provides sound leaders and good management in the safety effort.

It is important to note that the training program for supervisors includes human relations and communications skills. The supervisor is the link between upper management and the workforce. With proper training, supervisors can provide guidance, set a positive example, resolve problems, and identify the concerns of employees. Unless an orgnisation provides the necessary leadership training, it cannot expect to have effective leaders.

Developing the training program

The first step in developing a training program is to identify the needs of the audience and to develop program goals. Safety should be integrated into all job skill training from the beginning. A successful training program establishes sound course objectives that integrate training with production, quality, and cost-containment issues rather than viewing these as separate concerns.

Further, orgnisations cannot say that training has been provided if workers do not absorb the skill or knowledge being taught and cannot demonstrate competency. In such cases, the training is either incorrect or incomplete. The employer is responsible for providing appropriate, timely training that covers all pertinent safety issues within the orgnisation.

Program objectives

The first and most important step in developing a training program is to identify those who need instruction and to establish program objectives. The objectives must clearly state what students are expected to gain from the program. In order to do this, objectives must be measurable. Because employee attitudes and awareness generally cannot be measured, they are not considered proper training objectives.

Preparing course objectives requires training and practice. There is too much time and money at stake to allow a "hit or miss" approach. If students are to be taught a particular skill, the objectives must state the measurable level of performance desired. By detailing the program objectives, instructors can develop a training session to meet the company's established goals. Objectives also serve as a means of evaluating the training's effectiveness.

Weak or vague objectives often result in poor or unnecessary training programs. Excessively high objectives may overburden the students with useless information. With good course objectives, he students can focus on the essential requirements of the program. Prior to starting the objectives, management should review workers' responsibilities. The job description or job safety analysis (JSA) may provide the necessary information. A supervisor's job description may include the responsibility of training new workers in proper work methods. Thus, supervisors will need to receive education and experience in training skills. Orgnisations can make a costly mistake by assuming that everyone who knows how to perform a job also knows how to teach it. Teaching is a skill that requires not only training but practice and performance evaluations. A poor trainer can be the source of considerable problems in safety, quality, and production. As a result, the cost of not training the supervisors would most likely be far greater then the cost of a "train the trainer" program.

As safety and health issues become more complex, orgnisations must work hard to keep up with current requirements. Therefore, the objectives for training should be reviewed at least annually to ensure that they meet orgnisational needs. Many orgnisations are using the team approach to evaluate company training needs. The team may be comprised of members from the workforce, line supervision, safety department, maintenance, and management.

Supervisors and managers must demonstrate their support and approval of the training objectives. Workers are quick to detect when management support of a program is lacking. They will generally follow their supervisor's lead in either disregarding or adhering to safety procedures.

Training methods

Instructors can select one of several different training methods when preparing a program. Each method has strengths and weaknesses. The technique selected should be determined by the objectives to be met, type of student participation, time allocated, facility being used, and equipment available. Everyone learns at different speeds, and through different methods. Instructor must have the training and teaching skills to address these elements of human behavior. The following are the most common types of training techniques used in industry:

1. On-the-job training (OJT)
   a. Job instruction training (JIT)
   b. Over-the-shoulder coaching
2. Group techniques
3. Conference method
4 Individual techniques
5 Computer-assisted training (interactive).

On-the-job-training

On-the-job training (OJT) is widely used because it allows the worker to produce during the training period. However, this method has several drawbacks. As a result, when OJT is used, the following concerns must be addressed:

1. The trainer must posses proper training skills.
2. The training program should be developed to ensure that all workers are trained in the same way to perform their tasks in the safest and most productive fashion.
3. Adequate time is allotted to the trainer and trainee to be sure the subject is well covered and thoroughly understood.

Job instruction training

A variation of OJT is known as job instruction training (JIT), also referred to as the four-point method. Instruction is broken down into four simple steps:

1. preparation
2. presentation
3. performance
4. follow-up

This method of OJT has been highly successful. Workers are taught each job skill from a prepared schedule of training. The program is adjusted to each student so that workers learn one task before beginning the next.

In all training programs, the selection of the trainer is critical to program success. The one-on-one relationship between trainer and trainee allows for better control and communication. In the four-point methods, this trainer-trainee relationship works in the following ways;

Step 1 Preparation. During the preparation stage the instructor puts the workers at ease. He or she explains the job and determines what the worker currently knows about the subject. This stage also includes the preparation of the proper learning/working environment.

Step 2 Presentation. In the second step, the instructor demonstrates the work process. The student watches the performance and asks questions. The instructor should present the step in sequence and stress all key points.

Step 3 Performance. In the next step, the worker performance the task under close supervision. The instructor should identify any discrepancies in the work performance and note good performance. The worker should explain the steps being performed. This ensures that the student cannot only perform the task but understands how and why the task in done.

This stage continues until the instructor is satisfied with the worker's competence at the job.

Step 4 Follow-up . The final step is the follow-up of performance. The instructor and /or supervisor must monitor the worker's performance to be sure the job is being performed as instructed and to answer any questions the worker may have.

Of the various OJT methods, JIT is probably the most flexible and direct. Through coaching, the trainee is expected to develop and apply the learned skills in a typical work environment while under the guidance of a trained worker/trainer. The trainer must know the job thoroughly, be a safe worker, and have the patience, skill, and desire to train.

The advantages of training in the JIT method are:

1. The worker can be more easily motivated because the training/guidance is personal.
2. The instructor can identify and correct deficiencies as they occur.
3. Results of the training are immediately evaluated because the student is performing the actual job on actual equipment. The work performed can be judged against reasonable standards.
4. Training is practical, realistic, and demonstrated under actual conditions. Workers can easily ask questions.

Timing is an important element in this type of training. The trainee can receive help when needed, and the instructor can provide feedback as the training progresses. The instructor can also determine when the trainee is ready to move on to new levels of training.

It may be helpful to prepare a chart of tasks or subjects for which workers must receive training. This chart will make it easier to keep track of workers training progress and the levels of competence they achieve.

Of the other methods of OJT that can be used, the most common is known as over-the-shoulder coaching or the "buddy system". This system is considered effective in some situations, but has certain disadvantages:

1. Instructors may be selected for their availability rather than for their training skills. A trainer who lacks basic teaching skills can undermine the entire orientation of a new worker.
2. Each instructor may have his or her own way of performing the tasks being taught. This lack of continuity can make it difficult to control hazards in the workplace and lead to many accidents.
3. Key elements of orientation may be overlooked in the training program; many are not realise until an incident occurs.
4. Poor techniques or bad habits may be spread form one worker to another. Short cuts or safety violations are often demonstrated to new workers as the "way we do it."
5. Safety performance may not be emphasised during the training. Job performance should never be separated from safety standards in any training provided to workers.

Group techniques

Group techniques encourage participation from a selected audience. These methods allow trainees to share ideas, evaluate information, and become actively involved in the planning and implementation of company policy.

Several types of group training are used, but all require skilled facilitators to be successful.

Conference method

The conference method of teaching is widely used in business and industry. The reason this method is so readily accepted is because of the knowledge each participant brings to the group. In this process, the instructor controls the flow of the session as the participants share their knowledge and experience. The skill of the facilitator can mean the success or failure of these sessions. Facilitators must use various techniques to draw information and opinions from members. The number of people involved should be limited to allow open discussion from all participants. The opinions of each member should be recorded, and a summary of the group conclusions provided.

The conference technique is a valuable tool in problem solving. There are several situations where a safety and health professional may use the knowledge and expertise of members of the orgnisation to address safety and health issues. It is important that at the beginning of the conference, members identify their goals and expectations for the session. For example, if a conference has been called to identify possible solutions to a safety and health concern, the group must understand that they are to make recommendations only, not to establish policy or procedures. By defining the actual role of the conference at the start, the groups can avoid misconceptions and misdirection. When a groups is asked to make recommendations, they should be kept informed of the results of those recommendations.

If management fails to establish these ground rules and to provide follow-up information, the members may feel their efforts are ineffective. On the other hand, proper control and guidance of a conference can ensure its success and make it a gratifying experience for the participants.

Policies and attitudes in worker training

Teaching at the adult level

Instructors must always keep in mind that workers are adults and must be treated accordingly. It is generally agreed that the most accepted method for teaching adults is through the student interaction. As a result, orgnisations should limit group size to allow for student participation and response. Training must emphasise that safety is not a separate job to be done if and when other responsibilities permit the time. Rather, the supervisor must always consider how to maintain the production schedule with safe work practices.

In this regard, workers most likely will reflect the attitudes of their immediate supervisors. When supervisors make safety an important element in job performance, it will be treated as such by the workers. On the other hand, if a supervisor sends a message that production is the only important consideration, workers will tend to ignore safety policies to maintain the production schedule. These messages are communicated more often by a supervisor's actions than by words or written instruction. For this reason, supervisor's training should include human relations and communication skills to make the person a more effective leader and role model.

Integrate safety into all training

When an orgnisation has a formal training program, safety training can easily be incorporated into the curriculum. To do so, the training professional and safety and health professional should work together closely to plan the activities. Training supervisory staff in safety issues in normally the primary concern of the safety professional. The mission of the safety professional is to educate the members of the orgnisation in all elements of the safety and health program.

In many instances, such a program may require several years to educate and modify workers' existing attitudes toward "safety". However, integrating safety into production training will help to accomplish this goal. When supervisors are educated in leadership techniques, they become a strongly for the safety and health program. In the same sense, almost everything taught in safety and health program has a positive effect on production.

Safety training, like performance training, is most effective when it is provided on a continuing basis. This will test the creativity of training department staff. The dynamic, changing nature of the working world requires a constant review and updating of training programs. When instruction lacks imagination or stimulating materials, workers quickly lose interest in both the medium and the message.

Training new employees

Safety training begins when a new worker is hired. The person is usually open to ideas and to information about the way the company operates. From the first day, the new employee formulates opinions about the management, supervisors, fellow workers, and the orgnisation. Personnel managers may say they have never hired a worker with a bad attitude. This may not to be entirely true, but most employees' negative attitudes are developed after they have been on the job.

Timeliness of instruction can become a key issue in the orientation program. For example, although statistical data differ, it is generally agreed that new employees are significantly more prone to work-related accidents. This fact is attributed to the inexperience of new workers, their unfamiliarity with procedures and facilities, and their over zealousness to do the work. There are also a significant number of workers injured between the four-to-six-year range. This is generally attributed either to a change in work duties (new or transferred employee) or worker complacency. These issues can be covered in an ongoing training program and help to reduce the number of accidents.

The following subjects are suggested as part of the orientation program.

- company orientation: history and goals
- policy statements
- benefit packages
- organised labor agreements
- safety and health policy statement
- acceptable dress code
- personnel introductions
- housekeeping standards
- communications about hazards
- personal protective equipment
- emergency response procedures: fire, spill, etc.
- accident reporting procedures
- near-miss accident reporting
- accident investigation
- lockout/tagout procedures
- machine guarding

- electrical safety awareness
- ladder use and storage
- confined space entry
- medical facility support
- first aid/CPR
- hand tool safety
- ergonomic principles
- eye wash and shower locations
- fire wash and shower locations
- fire prevention and protection
- access to exposure and medical records.

This is by no means a complete list of the training needed to properly safeguard new workers. However, the subjects mentioned cover essential information that is far too important to overlook or leave to casual learning. A formal program should be developed not only to provide the worker with this information, but to create a strong link between employees and the safety and health orgnisation.

Many of these subjects are left to the supervisor to cover with employees when they arrive at the worksite. The supervisor must have time cover these points with the employee. Unfortunately, the importance of going over these subjects with the employee is not recognised until and accident occurs.

The supervisor should be current with the information present to new workers to avoid the age-old problem of contradicting the training material. Supervisors should also become involved in the development of training programs to work demands.

When supervisors start disregarding or contradicting the training program, the entire program-and the company's image-lost credibility with the workers.

The supervisor should re-enforce the training program and enhance the information by demonstrating how it will apply to the worker's specific job assignment. For example, the new employee may have been taught how to read the warning labels on chemical containers. The supervisor can then enhance this information by conducting a tour of the department, pointing out all hazards materials, and identifying the protection provided through personal protective equipment and control measures.

3

Safety Responsibilities

Safety, in the context of this chapter, concerns workplace health hazards and workplace accident prevention with special reference to the laws of the United States. Today's safety duties are often, but not always, combined with security and safety department.

The noun *safety* has been defined as

1. quality of being safe; freedom from harm or danger.
2. device to prevent injury.

In practice safety has been used extensively in place of, and interchangeably with, *hazard* or *protective*. Protective equipment is often titled "safety equipment." Hazard identification is called "safety inspection". Safety activities are usually planned to influence injury and illness directly by reducing both. It is generally understood that safety, however desirable, is temporary quality or condition easily.

Accident reduction involves an understanding of the various factors involved.

The critical stage, is creation of accident risk. A near-miss accident, which may be avoided by chance or the influence of an outside agency or condition. may not be recognized or understood. Failure to recognize risk invites repetition of the act until such time as an accident does take place. Supervisors or managers must be alert to ignorance and error as well as to those operations that, over time, might result in accident. An accident can lead to personal, property, and production loss.

Injuries in highway construction have caused concern in several areas: heavy equipment injuries, hot tar injuries, cement injuries, traffic accidents, and toxic fume inhilation from acids used. Excavating, trenching, and backfilling result in many serious cave-ins.

Furniture manufacturing has particular safety problems. Noise levels about 90 decibels are potentially damaging. Dust levels can cause cancer. Explosive dust particles are highly combustible. Rotating blade teeth and rotating knives are very hazardous.

Accidents are thought to result from failures of various types. Five causes of accidents are deficiency in technical data, organizational problems, failure of material, design deficiency, and natural phenomena.

Environmental hazards include any substance or energy not controlled properly in the workplace. One class of environmental threat includes toxic fumes, certain forms of dust, germs, explosive, and chemicals dangerous to human life and health. Another class is mechanical and includes unsafe or poorly shielded equipment. A third class is structural and includes poor construction and hazardous layout of the workplace.

Carcinogens are a major health hazard and safety concern. Abnormal reproduction of cells result from exposure to carcinogens. Benign tumors will not divide; malignant tumors will divide and, thus, spread. Cancers can result from environmental factors. For example, chemical carcinogens can enter the body in three ways. The term "latent period" describes how long it takes until the results of a carcinogen are detected. Some take 10 to 20 years to detect.

Occupational exposure to inorganic arsenic is very hazardous. This toxic substance is used to smelt ore into high-grade steel, gold, and copper. Arsenic is also used in preserving woods and producing pesticides. Polyvinyl chloride has been linked to cancer of the liver. No longer produced, it has been used in pipes, liners, and electrical equipment shielding.

Sabotage or other deliberate criminal acts may also create accidents but are outside our accident flow systems. Arson, bombing, and other terrorist acts are essentially criminal, whether perpetrated by participants in a labour dispute, by criminals, or by political terrorists.

Good and poor housekeeping have important effects on injury and illness. Good housekeeping practices relate to keeping paths clear, replacing burned-out illumination, preventing the buildup of waste materials and contaminants, and associated concerns. Preventative maintenance complements good housekeeping. Machine guards, electrical grounds, and restraining devices must not be allowed to break down through neglect. Protective clothing, barriers, and respiratory gear need regular inspection and maintenance. Monitoring equipment deserves special attention and care.

The first U.S. factory inspection legislation was enacted in the State of New York. Prior to the mid-1800s, the European guild system, with its closely supervised training for apprentices and journeymen by master craftsmen, minimized accidents and hazards. The Industrial Revolution, with its earliest development in England, reached rapid development about 1880. Workers were ill prepared for their employment: skill deficiency or incomplete understanding of the task is a major cause of accidents, and workdays averaging 11 to 13 hours increased accident potential. Facilities for medical care were inadequate, and professional medical was help seldom available. Injured workers received little compensation. Death due to job injury meant a small donation to the widow and funeral expense payment.

As American industrial development intensified, it was accompanied by technological advances, many of which created new safety hazards. Moving machinery and toxic and flammable materials began to exact a heavy toll on workers' health. Coal mines presented other problems, and mine disasters culminated in legislation, first in Pennsylvania, to reduce risks to miners. Early factory inspection requirements lacked enforcement and acceptance. Voluntary compliance was limited.

Andrew Carnegie and John D. Rockefeller are credited with leading efforts in safety, beginning in the last decade of the nineteenth century. Their managers were told to reduce all types of waste. Loss of workers due to preventable accidents was viewed by some managers as unnecessary waste due to the costs of replacing and training a new worker.

Workmen's compensation laws for those injured due to work hazards or conditions were stimulated in the early decades of the twentieth century-when industry surveys disclosed a very high level of worker death and injury at that time. Certain industries posed special problems, for example, the match manufacturers and the plumbing products and paint manufacturers. The present National Safety Council was created during this period and was given the task of gathering statistics and aiding industry to increase safety measures.

War always leads to the development of materials with civilian applications. World War I was no exception: protective materials needed for combat troops exposed to poisonous gas were later incorporated into the American workplace. The necessity for uninterrupted high production that attends any war led to competitive safety-related awards. During this period, the U.S. Supreme Court affirmed employer responsibility for work-related injury and accident, although lower courts often failed to authorize compensation in specific cases.

New federal safety codes were signed into law during the 1930s. The Walsh-Healy Public Contracts Act, passed in 1936, required those companies performing government contracts to eliminate dangerous, hazardous, and unsanitary conditions. During World War II, much of American industry were enjoying government contracts and was thus required to follow the regulations of the Walsh-Healy Act. The U.S. Department of Labour published minimum health and safety standards in 1942. It was at this time that safety became recognized as a full responsibility. During World War II, accidents in industries were aggravated by the influx of new, untrained workers hired to replace drafted workers to raise production for war needs of America and her allies. A steady improvement in safety programs served to decrease injury rates after the first few years of World War II.

Injury rates continued to decline until the 1960s, when the trend reversed sharply. Safety personnel and consumer advocates have disagreed on the cause of the new higher injury rates. Safety practitioners have explained that the dangers created by new machinery and processes are not well understood by inexperienced workers. Ralph Nader, the most prominent of the consumer advocates, emphasized industry shortcomings in carrying out safety laws and cheating in reporting lost-time injuries. The American consumer movement reached a peak during the late 1960s. Much legislation was enacted, and labour unions were stimulated to campaign for improved workmen's compensation laws. Safety specialists recognize 1968 as the year that the National

Safety management Society was organized. Promotional literature of this group emphasizes the possible increase of business efficiency through application of loss-minimization efforts.

Federal safety legislation reached its greatest expansion during the 1960s as well. Laws include the Water Quality Control Act of 1965, the Federal Metal and Nonmetallic Mines Safety Act of 1966, the Air Quality Act of 1967, the Fire Research and Safety Act of 1968, the Construction Safety Act of 1969, and, the most famous and far-reaching, the Occupational and Safety Act of 1970.

A variety of governmental and nongovernmental agencies have responsibility for enforcing national safety standards and/or making recommendations to industry. Included are the Occupational Safety and Health Administration, the National Fire Protection Association, the Department of Transportation, the Environmental Protection Agency; and the Mine Safety and Health Administration.

The William-Steiger Occupational Safety and Health Act went into effect April 20, 1971. The Occupational Safety and Health Administration is located in the Department of Labour. OSHA sets job safety and health standards, providing inspectors to enforce the standards. Priorities for inspection are catastrophies and fatal accidents, valid employee complaints, random selection of establishments for inspection, and target industry and target health hazards. Industries targeted as having the highest accident frequency rates include maritime, meat and meat products, roofing and sheet metal, lumber and wood products, and transportation equipment. Health hazards of the highest priority have been asbestos, carbon monoxide, cotton dust, lead, and silica.

The most frequently violated accident standards are

1. Electrical grounding
2. Abrasive wheel machinery
3. Welding, cutting, braizing
4. Floor patterns and exit marking
5. Mechanical power-transmission pulleys
6. Fire extinguishers
7. Material handling belts

The most violated construction safety standards are

1. Posting safety notices
2. Housekeeping
3. Guarding open boundaries
4. Head protection
5. Grounding requirements

OSHA violations result in citations, although, under certain circumstances, temporary orders may allow variance from an OSHA standard. Citations describe violations and fix a time for removal of the condition or correction of the hazard. Employers may contest citations. The secretary of the Department of Labour has the authority to assess penalties, which may be contested.

The National Fire Protection Association, organised in 1896, is an international nonprofit grown with national headquarters in Boston, Massachusetts. It is not responsible to any government or other regulatory agency. Technical fire protection and prevention standards are issued by NFPA, and they have been widely accepted and used by government and industry. *National Fire Codes,* compiled in 15 volumes and issued annually, contain codes, standards, and recommended practices. Other NFPA publications include the *Fire Journal*, NFPA *Inspection Manual*, and *Fire Protection Handbook.*

The U.S. Department of Transportation was established at the cabinet level in 1966. It develops and coordinates programs to provide safe, economical, and efficient transportation on land and sea and in air. There are seven major divisions in DOT:

1. The Federal Aviation Administration deals with safety of civil aviation.
2. The National Transportation Safety Board oversees marine, highway, pipeline, and civil aviation to investigate accident causation and appropriate corrective measures.
3. The Federal Highway Administration has jurisdiction over the safety of motor carriers.
4. The Federal Railroad Administration sets and enforces safety standards for railroads.
5. The National Highway Traffic Safety Administration sets vehicle standards and designs highway traffic safety programs.
6. The U.S. Coast Guard inspects and certifies merchant vessels and licenses civilian seamen.
7. The Urban Mass Transportation Administration helps to provide and improve mass transportation facilities.

The Environmental Protection Agency was instituted in 1970. It represents 15 federal programs and was formed to attack serious pollution problems including those relating to air, water, and noise.

The Mine Safety Health Administration was created in 1973 in the Department of the Interior. It administers provisions of the federal Coal Mine Health and Safety Act of 1969 and federal Mine Safety and Health Act of 1977. Congress recognized that death and serious injuries to coal miners are serious problems and a need to improve working conditions in the mines was overdue. MSHA carries out programs of enforcement, assessment of civil penalties, and training for mine operators and miners. Much of MSHA inspection, citation, and appeal procedures parallel those of the Occupational Safety and Health Act. In the case of imminent danger, an authorized representative of the MSHA can issue an order that mandates the removal of all personnel in a mine or mines and prohibits future entry until the danger is past. Employers may be fined for deliberate violation of safety standards. Miners may be fined for smoking violations. Equipment suppliers are liable for penalties if such equipment fails certain specifications or regulations.

National workmen's compensation legislation allows workers or their survivors compensation for occupational injury or disease "arising out of" and "in the course" of employment. Outside the United States, workmen's compensation has sometimes been replaced by a national insurance plan. Germany initiated workmen's compensation in 1884; the United Kingdom passed a similar law in 1894. Various American states followed suit soon after. National statutes relating to workmen's compensation include the Federal Employee's Compensation Act, Longshoreman's and Harbor Worker's Compensation, and provisions of the federal Coal Mine and Safety Act relating to black lung disease. Not all workers in the United States are covered by workmen's compensation. Some categories not include are farm workers and domestic workers. Each state has its own law, and provisions vary. *Controversy* surrounding workmen's compensation usually deals with the high *premium* cost that must be borne by industry and the increasingly higher benefits that are paid to disabled workers. Costs sustained by industry under these acts have persuaded many to increase concern for safety.

Some highlights of the Pennsylvania workmen's compensation legislation are presented now for the purpose of example.

1. Employers should post a list of five physicians authorized to treat injured or ill employees.
2. Employers should provide emergency medical care if needed and transportation to nearby medical facilities.
3. Employers must promptly investigate every injury to employees.
4. Workmen's compensation is no fault. An employee gives up rights to recover from the employer through legal action other than workmen's compensation.
5. Compensation is not paid it an injury or death is ruled self-inflected or caused by a law violation on the injured's part.

As this point it is necessary to question why so much federal legislation has been enacted to promote safe working environments and reduce health hazards. If common sense and logic argues for the reduction of any unnecessary loss, why has it been necessary to force American commercial interests to take safety steps? The issue is complicated by the apparent ignorance of business management in respect to the cumulative effect of those losses. Many may be delayed, such as for example, black lung disease. Business accounting has traditionally shunned the effort necessary to identify loss elements contributing to safety overhead. This quantitative failure applies also to other WAECUP losses. The personnel most closely involved, the loss-control practitioners, must do the necessary investigation and research leading to a cataloging of costs involved. Precise estimation or audit of dollars lost to the corporation due to a safety or security problem must be made.

Legislation and regulation, inspections and penalties, will not achieve desired safe and hazard free environments. Only voluntary compliance by management and labour will succeed.

Management needs a commitment to the safety component of loss control. Without such commitment, laws are seen as adversary acts by management that seeks to evade or delay regulations wherever possible. Managements that support safety compliance publicly but avoid its responsibilities privately play a dangerous game indeed, for the accident risk can easily result in double loss: the losses common to any injury or accident and the fines and civil liability incurred for noncompliance with safety laws and regulations.

Voluntary compliance requires education and training on an initial and continuing basis. management's role in a voluntary compliance program requires five actions:

1. Analysis of those government agencies having safety responsibilities toward the workers of a particular industry in a particular geographical location. Liaison will be initiated with representatives of their agencies to ensure mutual understanding of responsibilities in regard to safety and health. Such liaison is useful, periodically, when questions or problems arise.
2. A corporate policy statement setting out the organization's safety philosophy drawn up and distributed to management and labour.

3. Posting of media resources, such as posters and memoranda, to inform and remind all employees of their safety responsibilities.

4. Employee training, including a discussion of government standards and the responsibilities of management and workers.

5. Distribution of government standards and regulations to designated personnel for their use and reference.

A delegation of safety and health responsibilities needs to be made to ensure smooth functioning of voluntary compliance. Upper-level management has the ultimate responsibility, but it can delegate authority for establishing and operating a comprehensive safety and health program. Loss-control safety staffs have a responsibility to draft the details of such a plan and must implement the program. A method for evaluating safety results is necessary.

Midlevel line and staff are involved as each department head assumes a leadership role in gaining support for voluntary safety compliance among those workers assigned to the department. Front-line supervisors are the management personnel most directly involved compliance program, depending on their attitudes as well as on assistance and support from above.

Benefits of voluntary compliance are many. Those listed below represent advantages available to a varying degree, depending on the success of the program:

1. Cost reduction
    - Human
    - Property
    - Workmen's compensation rates
    - Wasted materials and products
    - Downtime and repair

2. Enhanced employee satisfaction
   Morale benefits
   Job satisfaction
   Good employee relations
   Fewer union grievances
   Lower absenteeism
   Less turnover

3. Reduced government interferences
   Fewer citations
   Reduced likelihood of penalties
   Fewer inspections
   Reduced resources on administrative matters
   Fewer hearing and court appearances

Voluntary compliance also involves committee formation. Safety and health committees assist line employees in active promotion of safety. Responsibility remains with management, and authority for the safety program belongs to the safety staff. Safety and health committee assist by pointing out potential hazards and by suggesting how challenges can be met wisely and economically. This is an advisory role. Key personnel, not necessarily supervisors, from all departments affected by the safety and health plan should be on the committee. Some line employees are needed to provide balance. Union representation is always necessary. Committees should normally be as small as possible, consistent with requirements. Large committees function with difficulty if at all.

Loss-control safety staff has a major responsibility for awareness and training to promote the voluntary compliance plan. New employee training should cover (1) operations of the corporation, (2) company policy on safety and health, (3) potential hazards in respect to environment, (4) materials and equipment, (5) safety protective equipment required and recommended, and (6) the process of reporting hazards and accidents.

Information, especially awareness training, is needed by corporate administrators, too. The safety staff represents more than a conduit leading at one end to workers and at the other to supervisors and administrators. Instruction and guidance must be given to both groups. Only in this way can the voluntary compliance program be successful in reducing accidents, injuries, and overhead. Specialized training, such as first aid and CPR techniques, are often performed by the American Red Cross and American Heart Association at little or no charge.

Refresher training in safety is recommended, especially when certain indicators are present. These include an increase in accidents or near misses, observed carelessness in use of protective equipment, disregard of mandatory safety procedures, and introduction of new workplace hazards.

As is the case for all loss-control problems, safety motivation presents serious challenge and is not clearly understood. The failure of the Highway Safety Administration and others to curb motor vehicle accidents or to encourage the use of seatbelts is a classic example of a continued failure to motivate the motoring public in regard to their own safety. Safety motivators that have had some apparent success include employee recognition, and praise, preferential job placement, and promotion. Recognition can take the form of cash bonuses, gifts, continued identification, or media publicity.

Record keeping plays a major part in modern safety programs. In many cases, there is a legal or insurance requirement for such records. However, records, whether mandatory or not, are important measures of safety success and guidelines for safety program improvement. It is always important to create, maintain, and review records dealing with injuries and conditions.

A safety record-keeping staff must be identified within the corporation to establish reporting procedures and deadlines. Records must be distributed, copies field, and some retained by law for as long five years. liability, both civil and criminal, can be created by record-keeping failure.

Certain accident or injury record requirements are common to government agencies. All employers with more than ten full-or part-time employees must keep safety records. Such forms are to be completed for every recordable illness or injury.

Modern safety practitioners have advanced considerably from their early reliance on engineering science. Machine guards and protective gear are still important. Safe work procedures and first-aid training retain value. Inspections and audits to locate hazards continue to take place. Now, however, legal constraints and requirements have moved safety higher up the management ladder. All of loss control has moved away from tocus on physical concerns to embrace cost minimization through a systems approach heavily dependent on information transfer. Such a parallel between security and safety presents further evidence for combination of these vital activities.

A safety program in the 1980s that demonstrates a systems approach would include a number of interlocking components. Educational psychology, hazard identification, hazard removal, emergency services, data collection and analysis, legislative compliance, and software and hardware represent typical programmatic divisions.

Safety, and all of loss control, is dependent on a team effort and management support for success. Illness and injury may result from management decisions as well as line activities. The modern safety plan requires a great measure of support at all corporate levels. Management decisions must be available for review by the safety department lest these decisions create accident or environmental risks unrecognized by decision makers. This information flow will result only if formal distribution channels include the safety department. Both management and safety must recognize the same goals and work to achieve them.

Safety standards have been identified as they relate to "consensus standards," federal standards, and proprietary standards. Consensus standards are those adopted by nationally recognized standards-producing organizations such as the previously mentioned National Fire Protection Association. Federal standards are those adopted by OSHA and other federal agencies as a result of enabling legislation. Proprietary standards are issued by manufacturers and industry associations such as the Institute of Makers of Explosives and American Welding Society.

Standards may be horizontal, or both. General industry standards apply to all employers. Fire protection, electrical, and sanitation are examples. Special industry standards cover particular operations. They have been issued to several industries including maritime and construction.

Safety programs are judged most frequently by the injury/illness frequency rates in a particular corporation. This rating system developed because of influence exerted by insurance underwriters and workmen's compensation authorities who use such statistical data to set premiums. Governmental bodies that consider health and safety legislation use the injury/illness frequency rate also. Opinions are divided about using the rate as a sole or primary measurement criteria, since insurance rate pressures may lead to understatements of occurrences, expenses, and lost time.

Regulatory agencies often claim that the illness/ injury frequency rate will reduce as compliance with standards, rules, and regulations improves. Rate reduction leads to lower premiums and lower medical costs. Unfortunately, despite regulation and inspection related to regulation, frequency rates have increased with few exceptions. Safety management practices and practitioner competence level are not always equal to the challenge.

Failures are often due to problems in identifying hazards. Other mistakes result in incomplete accident investigation or reporting. Too often the forms used by a safety department are not tailored to the corporation; rather, they are furnished by an outside agency such as an insurance company or regulatory agency.

An alternative measure of safety programs involves measurement of total costs related to accidents rather than frequency rates. These costs must include more than injury/illness costs. Accidents that cause waste, error, or decreased production must be subjected to cost analysis. This total accident cost concept eliminates the potential of low injury/accident frequency masking large losses in other accident areas.

Many costs are not recoverable and, therefore, require special attention. Recoverable safety costs are usually limited to casualty, fire, health, and medical insurance reimbursements. Miscellaneous nonrecoverable personnel costs include substitute overtime, replacement hiring and training, investigation, and report preparation. Miscellaneous nonrecoverable property costs include damage to tools, equipment, materials,and products.

The National Safety Council has expressed the view that a comprehensive safety program is composed of certain elements:

1. Supervisory participation
2. Middle-management participation
3. Top-management participation
4. Engineering, inspection, and maintenance
5. Screening and training employees
6. Coordination of personnel and procedures
7. Accurate and complete record keeping
8. Employee motivation

First-line supervision is essential to success. Thus, the supervisors must be cooperative and enthusiastic toward safety. Supervisors can coach employees to avoid injury and/or illness. When an incident occurs, the supervisor is usually the closest management employee and has the best chance to learn the facts and prevent complications.

Middle-and top-management people usually establish the style or attitude of the enterprise. This is especially true in regard to safety procedures. Management must obey and insist on good safety practice.

Engineering, inspection, and maintenance represent practical attempts by safety personnel to reduced hazards to other employees created by raw materials, machinery, or the production process.

Screening and training employees involved an understanding of human limitations. Some individuals are physically unsuited to certain activities. For instance, low body weight or back problems are deficits for someone charged with heavy lifting duties. An asthmatic may suffer abnormal respiratory problems that could be aggravated by job circumstances. Orientation training provides the employee with an understanding of job-related safety practices and equipment Retraining introduces safety changes and refreshes the forgetful mind.

Coordination of personnel and procedures reduces misunderstanding and error. It prevent duplication and overlap.

Accurate and complete record keeping is the only means of evaluating the success and failure of safety programs elements. Such records form the basis for change and improvement.

Employee motivation recognizes the uncertainty of attitude, all important to employee actions in regard to safety and the manner in which those actions are executed.

Weapons safety is of particular importance to guard personnel. There are very few, if any, who cannot remember a gun safety slip that might easily have been tragic. Three places are involved: the job, the range, and the home and automobile, if the weapon is not secured at the workplace. Critics are divided on keeping a loaded gun in the home or transporting a loaded gun to or from the workplace. Avoiding the issue of personal guns, it is reasonable to require the duty gun to be unloaded at home or while being transported to and from the workplace. Use of an employer's weapon in an incident not related to employment could subject the employer to litigation. For this reason, guards should not be allowed to possess loaded employers' guns off duty.

Firing ranges require special safety precautions. It is a good idea to have a range officer certified by the National Rifle Association or the U.S. Association of Firearms Instructors and Coaches or other reputable certification body.

New combat shooting courses are becoming popular. But they often fail to satisfy elementary range safety. Extreme danger results in indiscriminate handling of guns and ammunition. Guns should not be handed over or accepted unless open to show a clear chamber.

Do not prop the gun up, Case, rack, or holster the gun. The oldest safety rule is still the most important: never point a gun at anyone or anything you do not intend to shoot. On the firing line, muzzles should point down range at all times. The range officer should be obeyed immediately and exactly. Safety considerations mandate that a guard carrying a gun be qualified to shoot it accurately.

On-the-job gun handling requires exceptional safety precautions. For the guard's safety the gun must be mechanically reliable, clean, and loaded with good ammunition. For the public's safety, the gun must be holstered or held so that it cannot be taken from the guard. The gun should not be fired if innocent people are likely to suffer injury or unless there is no other alternative to protect life. If two or more guards have guns drawn, it is important to establish zones of responsibility to avoid wild firing that may injure the innocent or one of the guards.

Developing safety programme

The company under discussion bottles and blends liquors. Its work force is approximately 450, including about 80 management and clerical employees. Hourly employees include labourers, forklift drivers, guards, and maintenance personnel. The plant is highly automated. Thee are many buildings. Labourers must take pre-exployment health exams including back X rays due to lifting activity required. The plant nurse supervises workmen's compensation claims, which are handled through self-insurance.

On-site liquor, tanks, holding form 30,000 to 100,000 gallons, are filed by incoming trucks. All tanks are equipped with flame arresters and explosion venting to reduce the risks of fire and explosion.

Safety is the responsibility of the industrial relations manager. Ongoing safety emphasis includes hearing conservation, safety shoes, and safety glasses. Records are kept of all injuries. A safety committee meets once a month to advise on safety matters. Membership of the safety committee is widespread and includes personnel from diverse departments, both management and labour. The plant manager, chief engineer, comptroller, security and fire protection manager, industrial relations manager, and plant nurse participate on the committee.

The plant manager has stated the objectives of the program as quality supervision of employee action, efficient utilization of company equipment, and detection of possible improvements. Emphasis is given to the responsibility of all managers and supervisors for success of the programme. There is an annual review of safety goals, which are set jointly by the plant and industrial relations manager. Current goals are to reduce lost-time accidents, injury requiring out-side medical care, and cost of accidents. Progress reports are prepared five times each year to evaluate goal satisfaction.

Communication on safety is enhanced by an awareness program. Posters and flyers are displayed throughout the plant. Each department has its own bulletin board, protected by a glass door. It is the responsibility of plant guards to post minutes from the monthly plant safety committee, progress reports, departmental accident summaries, hospital treatment summaries, and incident reports.

Safe working procedures are taught by immediate department heads and supervisors. Special training may be given by the industrial relations manager. A Cardio-Pulmonary-Resuscitation CPR course has been taught by the plant nurse. Fire brigade training is given to certain maintenance personnel by the security manager.

Purchase of safety-related equipment are evaluated by the plant engineer to ensure that specifications meet the standards. Personal protective equipment is issued if a supervisor or department head states the need. The maintenance department warehouses safety equipment.

The most frequent injuries at this plant are cuts, bruises, sprains, and strains. A full-time nurse is available during the day shift, which is the only one. The plant dispensary includes beds, bandages, stretchers, an oxygen pack, and pharmaceuticals. The plant has outside doctors on retainer. The dispensary is inspected annually be a medical doctor. All injuries must be reported to the nurse immediately. The nurse keeps records of all accidents.

Safety illumination is maintained by same-day bulb replacement through the Maintenance Department. Guards report outages. Doors and emergency exits are equipped with panic hardware.

Alarms exist for fire protection. A siren and paging system is used. Fire is a particular danger because of the large quantities of flammable liquid in storage. Alcohol vapors are present at all times due to storage and production. Employees may smoke only in designated areas. There is widespread use of special switches and lights since a mere 3.28% concentration of pure alcohol in the air can result in explosion. Only EX-type vehicles are used in warehouses, case houses, and palletizing departments. EX vehicles are designed so that they may be operated safely in atmospheres containing flammable or explosive vapors or dust.

An 8-inch fire line runs the length of this facility. It

is fed by well water and is connected to three tanks holding jointly over 650,000 gallons. Pumps are used to maintain fire line water pressure. All fire hoses are connected to the fire line. A wet sprinkler system with heat sensors is connected to the fire line. This system is tested weekly. Different sections of the fire line system are tested weekly also. Fire alarm bells are located on the exterior of each building and connect with the security office, which has a zone panel to identify the alarm location. The fire brigade reports to a central location where a vehicle waits to transport brigade members to the alarm location. Over 400 portable fire extinguishers are located in various buildings. These extinguishers are carbon dioxide and dry chemical. They are weighed and inspected annually.

4
Safety Adminstration

The victims of industrial accidents are, as often as not, members of a Trade Union. It is generally accepted that Trade Unions do a lot for their injured members—cash benefits, convalescent treatment, legal advice and assistance—but all this comes after the accident. What are Trade Unions doing to prevent industrial accidents?

Trade Unions exist to represent, protect, advice, and educate their members and to serve their interests generally. The responsibility for providing and maintaining safe working places and safe systems of work and for enforcing the system of work is a managerial responsibility. Any attempt to share that responsibility would create considerable legal and practical difficulties, and uncertainty as to where the responsibility lay would probably lead to more rather than fewer accidents.

The Unions are well aware of the mounting toll of industrial accidents, and of their cost in economic terms and in terms of human suffering and disability. Every year the concern of the Unions is reflected the proceedings of their Annual Delegate Conferences and of the Annual Meeting of the Trade Union Congress.

Trade Unions co-operate with Government Agencies and with employers in the investigation of the causes of industrial accidents and diseases. The history of British safety, health and welfare legislation is, in part, the history of the struggle of the Trade Unions to win legally defined minimum safety standards for their members.

It is indicative of the Trade Union attitude that the Unions agreed to mark the centenary of the first Trades Union Congress by providing funds to establish a permanent Institute of Occupational Health to discover and attack the causes of industrial diseases.

Trade Unions are in exactly the same position as any other body which provides a service in a free society. They have to order their priorities according to what the 'customer' wants. The accident are in a particular plant or industry may be bad, but if industrial relations generally are also had, it is not a bit of use a Trade Union officer talking to his members about co-operation to prevent accidents when his members have wages and working conditions on their minds. The effort to reduce the toll of accidents must be part and parcel of a combined effort to improve working conditions generally. Safety, health, and welfare are inseparable.

Accidents are a reflection of human error in one guise or another. No one wills or designs them. They cannot be tidily explained away. The contributing factors are innumerable and not always immediately obvious. How can one explain the unhappy combination of the boiling saucepan, the temporarily preoccupied mother, and the climbing child? This simple and sadly common domestic situation contains all the ingredients of industrial accidents the danger point, lack of proper supervision, and the unheeding or inadequately instructed victim.

Statistics published by the Chief Inspector of Factories show that we are most vulnerable in precisely those areas of activity within which mechanical guards, sophisticated rules for the performance of certain tasks, or the provision of protective clothing serve no purpose.

In other words, in those areas in which we have to rely most on human intelligence, forethought and caution. That more than half of the reportable accidents fall into this category reflects the failure of management to manage, and says very little for the quality of the training provided for men or management.

A serious preventive programme will inevitably call into question our systems of selection, induction, and supervision. In the altogether wasteful and unproductive business of war a great deal of intelligent effort is devoted to the task of selecting and training the right men for the job. The armed forces demand a high standard of fitness and intelligence, particularly in the case of those who are likely to be placed in positions of command. Many of us know from personal experience that this remains true even in the stress of war.

Modern industry inescapably presents hazards to health and safety, but how much real care is devoted to the task of selecting the right man for the job at shop-floor level in every instance?

Many unskilled, or semiskilled processes require a high degree of mobility of labour. Men are shunted from one job to another according to the exigencies of the hour. It is true that many of the processes are fairly simple such that child could be taught in 10 min. This is unobjectionable so long as there is some margin for initial error and the initiation is properly supervised, but so often the supervisor is preoccupied with production problems and has far too many employees to manage, and even when the supervision and induction are good, it is sometimes resented by the worker.

Supervision is very important but when the question of promotion arises, how much consideration is given to the candidate's physical and temperamental fitness for the job or to the effect he is likely to have on those under his supervision? To what extent are his personal views tested on the relationship between productivity and safety? How much careful and sympathetic study is devoted to the delicate problem of the connection between physical fitness—or the absence of it—and accidents?

A particularly shocking feature of our accident record is the number of young persons under the age of 18 whom we maim. Some people expect boys or girls to become responsible adults the moment they enter a factory gate. So do the youngsters themselves. It cannot be overemphasised that proper training and patient, intelligent supervision is essential in the case of young people if we are not to perpetuate bad working practices. Their initial induction into the world of industry should be an extension of the road drill they were taught in primary school, and we should drop like a ton of bricks on any adult worker who is caught either introducing youngsters to dangerous short cuts or who scoffs at safety rules and procedures in the hearing of youngsters.

One could go on endlessly listing problems of this nature but enough has been said to indicate the field to which attention should be paid if we are to get out of the president dilemma and tackle the accident problem afresh.

It is precisely in this field that the Unions can be of most use. They cannot initiate and enforce safe and efficient working practices, but if employers are to overhaul their procedures for selecting, training, supervising and promoting their employees, they will do so more smoothly and effectively if, at the outset, they consult the Unions and seek their co-operation and active participation. Co-operation implies a degree of partnership, and partners have to be consulted and their opinions and suggestions considered with patience and respect. It would be no use simply to confront the Unions with a programme of radical reform-no matter how well intended—and to expect them to endorse it without having had a say in the formative stages. Neither can one expect that such a programme would be agreed upon in its entirely without discussion, disagreement, and amendment. There is bound to be a conflict of ideas and interests, but a workable scheme will emerge if both sides conduct themselves according to the rules of diplomacy and not the rules of war, and are repeatedly reminded that the common aim is to improve standards of safety, health, and welfare.

Once the co-operation of the Unions has been sought and secured, it is need not be confined to simply underwriting the good intentions of the employer. Given any encouragement at all the Unions can persuade their members to accept changes which are in their interest and can educate them to be safely conscious. It is part of the built-in defensive mechanism of human nature that one tends to think that disaster is something that happens to the other fellow. The purpose of education in safe working practices is to demonstrate that disaster need not befall any of us if we learn that there are tow ways of doing most things—the right way and the dangerous way. Trade Unions have excellent educational facilities and can draw upon a wealth of talent and experience, but here again the emphasis should be on co-operation. Whenever possible training in safe working practices should be a joint exercise relating to specific industrial conditions, because each industry has its own help and safety problems and, to some extent, its own terminology. Joint educational activities will help convince the workers concerned that their employer and their Union really mean business—that the training courses and safety conferences and committees are not just pious exercises which, in the end, lead to nothing.

So far, this discussion has been confined to the role of the Unions as associations of employees representing their members' interests but not directly and personally affected. Accident prevention is a shop-floor problem and no amount of impersonal exhortation is going to solve it. Any scheme designed to make the workplace a safer place directly concerns shop floor personnel and, in some cases, may even affect their earnings or their prospects of promotion. Their willing participation is essential. The most vital part of the Union's function is to secure that participation and do demonstrate that the advantages are real and tangible.

Joint consultation at every stage and at every level is the key to progress. Employees should be diligently consulted and kept informed in the formative stages of preventive scheme. Thereafter, their representatives should meet representatives of management regularly and be free to discuss every aspect of accident prevention and to air their criticisms and suggests in the sure knowledge that what they say will receive careful consideration an that the hazards and malpractice to which they draw attention will be remedied.

Once the Safety Committee has been formed and is functioning, the day-to-day tasks of consultation should be the responsibility of the Safety Committee men. The Trade Union officer should remain in the background to be summoned as arbiter only when every other avenue of approach has been explores unsuccessfully. This unallowed worker/management relationship is really fundamental to a good safety programme because it breeds responsibility, trust, and mutual appreciation of both sides of the problem. It enables employees to influence directly and to understand the significance of managerial decisions in matters which affect their health and safety. It generates a positive will to accept the notion that safety is everybody's business. Joint consultation of this is good Trade Union practice. Trade Union officers exist to lead and service their members, not to wet-nurse them. There is a great deal more satisfaction to be had from leading active participants than from shepherding the apathetic. We cannot, however, rely solely on voluntary co-operation. It will be effective of statutory regulations to spur the sluggard and penalise the recalcitrant.

The Trade Union viewpoint can be summarised briefly. Any initiative designed to reduce the toll of accidents in industry deserves the closest possible co-operation of all Trade Unionists. Here at least is one field in which the respective interests of employers and employees doubtedly coincide. The motive of safety conscious employer may be largely economic, but should motives concern us so long as the result is the provision and maintenance of a safe and healthy workplace? In the pursuit of industrial safety there is no room for barriers, no place for the 'them and us' mentality. Joint consultation and effective co-operation aimed at curing industry of the accident malaise represents enlightened self interest at its best.

It is doubtful whether anyone would seriously dispute what had so far been said about the fuits of joint consultation and yet, oddly enough, both industry and the Trade Unions continue to accept to complicated and divisive system of compensating those who suffer industrial injuries. Accident prevention is bedevilled by common law claims for damages. It is doubtful whether such claims make any appreciable contribution to the prevention of accidents. There are those who argue learnedly and honestly that do argue learnedly honestly that they do, but the annually increasingly accident statistics and the never ending lists of action awaiting the judgement of the courts are effective arguments to the contrary. The system is divisive and, therefore, detrimental to the atmosphere of goodwill and mutual trust so essential to preventive measures because it is a contest, and retains something of the air of the medieval joust. It is not the business of the judiciary to prevent accidents but to determine the question of liability in any given case according to a body of legal principles based upon case and statute law. Judgement is given according to the evidence as it is presented in court—usually a long time after the event. Many cases which, on paper, appear to be cast iron certainties, have been lost because the plaintiff faltered under cross-examination or because his witnesses failed to live up to their proofs of evidence. Anyone who has had the delicate task of advertising injured workers can sympathise with their bewilderment and their sense of having been cheated.

National Insurance benefits may remove some of the hardship and sting, but it is still questionable whether any useful purpose is served by retaining a legal right when the remedy is deponent upoon so many fallible factors.

This is not written in a spirit of disillusionment. It is appreciated that many learned and courageous judges have wrestled with htis difficult branch of the law to achieve just and equitable decisions. Nevertheless, in practice, claims for damages remain something of a gamble and it is no disrespect to our legal system to hold that such a method of compensating the victims of industrial accidents does nto measure up to the need of a complex industrial society.

The greatest single contribution that could be made to our efforts to prevent accidents would be to lift the sytem of compensating the casualties of industry out of the realm of law of tort and to pay compensation without reference to liability. The dividing line between employers' liability and simple industrial hazard is often a matter of narrow legal technicalit and there is no logical reason why injured employees should have to rely upon contentious common law claims to seek restitution of their physical and financial loss.

It is hardly relevant to this discussion to consider alternative schemes. Suffice it to say that others have canvassed similar views, and reform is not only possible—but probable.

In the field of accident prevention the primary function of the Trade Unions is to co-operate and to educate. The verbatim proceedings of the Trades Union Congress confirm that this view is widely and officially held within the Trade Union movement. There is a reservoir of goodwill, but one must guard against creating the false impression that the tak is an easy one; anything worthwhile seldom is. There are many pitfalls for the unwary along the way. There are historically rooted suspicious and prejudices to be overcome. Trade Unions can go just as far as fast as their members will follow. Sometimes their members are cautious and sceptical and have good reason to be. In spite of the acknowledged difficulties there are grounds for optimism. If one disregards much publicised strikes and disputes, the evidence would seem to suggest that the hard logic of post-war economic difficulties is bringing both sides of indsutry closer together. There is a general movement towards employee participation in the management of industry, a development viewed with some alarm in quarters where the old legal concept of 'master and servent' still lingers. The vigorous pursuit of effective joint consultation in matters of health and safety could be doubtly useful as a means of achieving the objects of the Health and Safety at Work, etc., Act 1974, and as a neutral testing ground for the wider notion of worker participation.

5

Employee Attitude Towards Safety

It is obvious that means of gauging employee attitude toward safety in general and toward the plant safety programme in particular would be very helpful in guiding action to increase the effectiveness of the safety programme. If the reaction to each specific measure such as plant safety meetings, safety committee activities, safety bulletins, safety rule books and the like could be readily measured with fair accuracy, it would be very helpful to the prosecution of the safety programme. Many serious attempts as such appraisals have been made, and various means have been tried. There have been many disappointments, but enough success has been scored to indicate that it is well worth while to undertake such appraisals. Measures that have proven valuable are :

1. Reports from safety personnel
   a. *Safety inspectors*
   b. *Worker-safety committeemen*
   c. *Union representatives*
   d. *First-aid attendants*
2. *Foreman canvass*
3. *Sampling by personal contact*
4. *Suggestion systems*
5. *The safety inventory or questionnaire*

Reports from safety personnel

Inspectors full time on safety can, if stimulated to do so and properly instructed, sound out many fellow employees and report with fair reliability as to their findings. Also, if in their day-by-day inspection work, their attitude is receptive, they will receive many suggestions, hear many "gripes," and be asked many questions. It is best, however, to have them make verbal, rather than written, reports, because such personnel generally dislike "paper work." Also, written reports tend to become routine and to degenerate to meaningless forms. On the other hand, a personal report to a superior on the matter in question can be as complete and meaningful as the condition may justify. The inspector should be told why the information is wanted, how he should ask for it, and in general, whom he should ask. This method should not be over-used, else it will become farcical. Used occasionally through reasonably adept persons, it yields good results.

Safety committees of workmen are, at times and in favourable situations, valuable sources of information on the attitude of their fellow workmen toward safety. Workmen will usually talk freely to their fellows. This can frequently be made a part of their duties, but the amount of time and effort they will be in a position to spend for this purpose will usually not be great. Their services are usually most effective in connection with safety measures in which they have had a part and, therefore, maintain a personal interest.

Alert safety-minded union leaders and safety representatives can frequently furnish valuable information on the attitude of their membership toward the safety programme, or specific parts of it. When the relationship between the union leadership and the management is good, and when the union is actively cooperating with the company safety programme, the union can be particularly helpful in bringing safety "gripes" to light. Also, it can frequently be helpful in correcting mistaken employee attitudes.

First-aid attendants, particularly the plant nurse, can be especially helpful. A nurse who is understanding, friendly, and intelligent can determine, without too obviously trying to do so, the reaction of most of those who go to first-aid. Her attitude and questioning need not amount to more than a live interest in safety work. In so doing, she will inevitably produce a further profit by promoting interest in safety among many of those to whom she talks.

The foreman canvass

The foremen are in the key position in accident prevention because of their responsibility for, and intimate contact with, both the workmen and the details of the work. The are also in the best possible position to keep in touch with the attitude of those under them toward safety. However, this presupposes not only that the foremen themselves are keenly safety-minded, but that they are also active participants in the safety programme. They should have an active part in planning it, and must be kept well-informed on plans, expectations, and results. If these conditions are met, the foreman canvass becomes worth while and reasonably reliable. Very simply, it means the practice of having each foreman undertake in definite systematic fashion, at intervals, usually irregular, to ascertain the attitude toward the safety programme, or some specific phase of it, of each workman in his crew. It is best not to keep any records beyond such notes as the foreman may need in order to make his report, and it is usually best not to let the workmen know that even such notes are taken. An exception arises when a workman makes a suggestion for improvement, in which case proper credit should be given as a matter of record. Extensive detailed records are not ordinarily justified, though brief written summaries of the findings on each such canvass will be necessary to give the full picture. Since the purpose of the canvass is primarily to measure the current effectiveness of the safety programme, or of some phase of it, there is little point to keeping permanent records of the findings.

Sampling by personal contact

A safety director or safety engineer who is well-liked and "gets around" can sample a cross section of all personnel and reach reasonably reliable conclusions therefrom. He will, however, have to use considerable judgment to avoid being misled by persons unwilling to return an answer he might not like. Also, he must keep his powers of analysis uninfluenced by wishful thinking. Properly done however, his sampling can be a very useful check on, and supplement to, other means of testing employee attitude.

Suggestion systems

The use of suggestion systems to bring to light employee ideas for improvements in processes, methods, or equipment has long been a fairly common practice. They are similarly usable in the interest of safety, and when so used, they can be very helpful in determining employee attitude toward specific safety measures. Suggestions and comments may be invited on means of improving safety meetings or safety contests or the inspection procedure, etc. Criticisms may be asked for, and if answered in the plant newspaper or on the bulletin board, may provoke further suggestions are ideas of value.

Attitude surveys

Employee attitude surveys to find out what the employees think about their company, their supervisors, and their working conditions are rather widely used. Most of them include some questions on safety. A few have been devoted wholly to safety and closely allied working conditions. Out of a great amount of experimentation have come effective techniques that, properly applied under favorable conditions, will bring reasonably reliable results. However, experience indicates that such surveys will be of doubtful validity if undertaken during periods when:

1. There have been mass layoffs or discharges.
2. There are a large number of hirings.
3. Major changes in the company's organiz-ational structure are underway or recent.
4. Employees are restless or dissatisfied.
5. Union organization drives are on, or union negotiations are underway.
6. Major changes in plant or processes are underway.

The majority of such surveys attempt to cover all employees in the given plant or group. In nearly all cases, a written questionnaire is used for this purpose. However, many surveys are made by a sampling process that is more frequently handled by personal interview than by a written questionnaire. Although, in many cases, the survey is made by the staff of the personnel department, the more usual practice is to employ and outside specialist for the purpose, either a professional firm or an university research group. The weight of opinion as expressed by companies who have made use of attitude surveys appears to be heavily on the side of using an outside agency, partly because of the specialized experience and skills obtainable thereby, and partly because of the greater assurance this gives that the approach will be unbiased and objective. This course also gives greater assurance of complete anonymity, where that is desired. There is nearly unanimous agreement that anonymity is necessary in attitude surveys dealing with controversial matters (particularly how the employee is treated by his supervisor), but since safety is not, or at least should not be, a controversial matter, many feel that anonymity is not necessary. Certainly, if an employee raises a safety point on which he is misinformed, or if his comment indicates a wrong attitude, it is helpful if the matter can be "thrashed out" with him face to face. However, through discussions at safety meetings, announcements on bulletin boards, or articles in the plant newspaper, such anonymous comments and complaints can usually be taken care of just as is common practice with unsigned suggestions received through a suggestion system.

The survey conducted annually for a number of years by the Springfield, Mass. plant of the Westinghouse Co. shows that if properly handled in a plant where management and employee relations are good, valuable results can be had even though the employees are urged to sign the questionnaires. Since these are handed out to each worker individually by the foreman, few failed to sign. As would be expected, it eventually became largely a rehashing of answers previously made and was discontinued. It did indicate, however, that safety is so infrequently controversial, that anonymity is less important than being able to discuss each answer with the employee who gave it. The two following paragraphs are quoted from a talk given by a plant executive.

The westinghouse safety inventory

"In order to promote full employee cooperation, the inventory is well-publicized in the plant in advance and is carried out following the annual year-end stock inventory. This emphasizes the inventory idea and the use of the findings in planning the safety programme for the ensuing year. When the working force returns after the inventory shut-down, each foreman or other supervisor hands a card and an instruction sheet to each member of his force with the earnest request that he take stock of his job and surroundings with regard to safety, fill the card out fully, sign it, and turn it in. Salaried workers are included in this distribution. the degree of employee compliance secured is indicated by the fact that, in a typical year, out of 2025 cards distributed, 1904 were returned completely filled out. The answers to many of the questions furnished valuable clues to needed action. In many cases, the answers revealed the need of more and better guarding, or of more personal protective equipment. Obviously, each guard lack discovered by this means reflects on the inspection service or upon the foreman, or both. Each protective equipment. Obviously, each guard lack discovered by this means reflects on the inspection service or upon the foreman, or both. Each protective equipment lack reflects on the safety engineer or the foreman, or both. Many such cases brought to light through any one inventory calls for a tightening up of inspection, as well as more attention to safety by at least the foremen involved. If many of the hazards pointed out were previously known, it indicates a need for prompter corrective action.

"Answers to the question, 'Do you wear safety shoes?' brought out the fact that many who should have been wearing them were not doing so, also that this was at least partly due to poor fitting and lack of knowledge of the protection they afford. This indicated the need of more attention to fitting, and also called for a better sales job. The safety engineer would have discovered this condition had he carried out a foot hazard survey either by itself, or as part of a survey covering all types of personal protective equipment. It is good practice to include such items in the job standards. If no job standards have been established, the need should be determined by the safety engineer in consultation with the foreman or department superintendent. If there is no safety engineer, this responsibility should be placed on the foreman or department head, in consultation with the safety committee, if there is one."

Questions designed to direct employee attention to specific key facts also proved to be valuable. For example, the two questions, "Where is the nearest fire alarm box?" and "Where is the nearest stretcher?" aroused a great deal of interest, much hunting them out and much pacing off the distances.

The question, "What improvements do you recommend?" brought many valuable suggestions, covering a wide range. The need of an improvement in certain safety equipment was indicated by 18 out of 96 suggestions from the 1938 inventory. There were many recommendations for better lighting and better ventilation. These were accepted as indicative of a need for better application of recognized standards of god practice in these two important items.

The wisdom of asking such question as, "Does your work make you nervous or over-fatigued?" may be questioned. Older workers whose powers are failing may fear to admit such adverse effects lest it lead to shifting to a lower paid job or a lay-off. Also, such a question is an invitation to the hypochondriac. Finally, it is often difficult to distinguish between such conditions caused by the work and by of-the-job activities and tensions. Somewhat similar comments apply to the question, "Do you experience any physical ill effects from your work?" However, despite these limitations on the value of these questions, 75 affirmative answers were received to the first, and 84 to the second. Investigations of the conditions involved in the complaints showed that a substantial proportion were justified and suitable corrective action was taken.

Many would question the validity of the question, "Do you know the company's safety rules?" because a moment's reflection would lead the employee to realize that a negative answer would almost certainly result in his being bothered or pushed into learning them. The "wise" ones would answer "yes." The effective way to find out who knows the rules is to quiz the employees on the rules themselves. The result, 1409 affirmative, 74 negative, bears this out. The question, "Do you believe that the safety rules should be enforced?: is also subject to a large factor of uncertainty, because workers would tend to give what they believe to be the desired answer. The fact that, in this instance, there were only 70 negatives, together with the fact that more answered this question than answered the preceding one, supports this opinion.

A modification of the safety inventory idea has been used early in the safety programme by limiting it to safety committee members, or other key men. In one plant, after its workmen's safety committees had been functioning for about a year, each committeeman was asked to "inventory" safety conditions in the area he represented. Each used a standard list of common hazards, supplemented by the hazards peculiar to his area. The results of these inventories were discussed in safety committee meetings and advisable corrective action was decided upon.

The revere safety test

Revere Copper and Bras, Inc., in cooperation with Syracuse University, has developed a very interesting method of testing worker-safety knowledge. This test makes use of a pamphlet containing 54 sets of pictures, each depicting god and bad practices based on rules in the rule book, a personal copy of which is given to each employee when he is hired, and which he is expected to master.

Each testee is given a copy of the picture pamphlet and answer sheet having 54 sets of small squares numbered to correspond to the sets of pictures. He is directed mark an "x" in each square corresponding to a picture in which a picture in which a safety rule is violated.

Revere started the use of this test in 1945. An official reports that it has proved to be valuable in testing both employees who have lost-time accidents and employment. He does not recommend for hiring those applicants scoring less than a certain level. He divides the scores above that minimum into five levels, which indicate the extent of safety instruction needed. He considers the use of this test have been "a large contribution factor" in halving the company injury rate during the years 1945 to 1951 inclusive.

Safety surveys for job applicants

The survey idea may be used to determine the attitude of job applicants toward safety as well as other toward other matters. Summarization of the returns from over 500 applicants who filled out questionnaire cards at a plant in New England showed in part:

1. 42 per cent considered safe working conditions of first importance, 49 per cent put wages first. The remaining 9 per cent were scattered or indefinite.
2. 34 per cent believe each plant should have safety rules that each employee should know and obey.
3. 63 per cent believed that the employees should have a part in developing the safety rules.

4. 24 per cent liked the idea of suggestion boxes and rewards for safety ideas, whereas 21 per cent considered them a nuisance or a subterfuge.

5. 30 per cent thought safety was almost wholly to the workmen themselves. 14 per cent didn't think that employers cared whether their workmen were hurt or not, and 48 per cent hadn't thought much about safety.

6. 54 per cent reported that they had never been given any safety instruction. 27 per cent said "a little," and only 14 per cent said they had received careful safety training.

The B & O railroad company safety quiz

The B & O Railroad Company safety quiz is an excellent example of an employee-safety survey so handled that response is wholly voluntary. It is started off by a personal letter from the president to each of the approximately fifty thousand employees. The letter emphasizes the company's strong concern for the safety of its employees, solicits their full cooperation in protecting their own safety and that of fellow employees, and specifically asks that the questionnaire to follow be filled out and returned in the stamped, addressed envelope that accompanied it. Some of the questions were designed as thought provokers, others to check on the safety programme.

The question, "Would you speak to a fellow employee you saw violating a safety rule?" is of the first type. More than nine out of ten who answered said they would. A sound approach to safety was indicated by the heavy majority for (1) in the question, "Which is these statements is most true?"

1. Accidents are bound to happen

2. Accidents can be prevented

There are, in all, 20 questions of the multiple-choice or best-answer type. Each employee is requested to check his answers without fear or favor and "not to sign his name unless he wants to." No space is provided for a signature.

Survey specialists report that for so far flung an organization so scattered geographically, the 16% response obtained is very good for a purely voluntary, mailed questionnaire of this sort. Although more pressure would have brought a greater response, the close contact and follow up used in the East Springfield survey would be unduly expensive on a great railroad system.

Value of safety surveys

The East Springfield officials value the safety inventory highly. Their experience appears to justify the conclusion that, properly set up and handled, such inventories should be valuable in checking on the effectiveness of any well-established and reasonably well-functioning safety programme. Good employee cooperation is obviously basic to success. This cooperation could not be expected in a plant in which at least reasonably good attention had been given to the elimination of physical hazards. In other words, the inventory is, as its name implies, a means of finding flaws, weaknesses, defects, and lacks in performance that is already good.

The use of the safety inventory early in a safety programme in order to get the employees' viewpoint and foster their interest is, at best, highly questionable. It would obviously be more difficult to get good employee cooperation, but, if it were gotten, a flood of recommendations too great to be taken care of with reasonable promptness would probably result. It would seem to be much sounder to reserve this device for use chiefly as a check up. Most unsafe conditions and hazardous practices are discoverable by plant inspection, job analysis, accident investigation, and cause analysis. Safety committee activities play a large part in this picture. Suggestion systems, properly set up and maintained, bring in additional valuable ideas and foster further employee cooperation.

The B & O management also finds its safety quiz valuable in bringing out ideas and viewpoints of at least those employees who take the trouble to fill out the questionnaire and return it. Obviously, these are, in general, the more safety-minded employees and, therefore, their ideas should be of real value. That this is actually the case is shown by the numerous points made that the management quickly acted upon. These points included the conduct and coverage of safety meetings, action on safety matters, the effectiveness of various elements of the safety programme, and the validity of various safety rules. There was so much of value, that a careful analysis of the returns was made and a detailed report thereon was transmitted to all top supervisors throughout the system.

With regard to the use of the Revere test, the careful appraiser is naturally cautious in questioning the soundness of a conclusion based on such experience and accomplishment. However, the validity of such a test in determining the employability of applicants is at least questionable. Its value in showing the need of safety instruction is obvious. The fact that a number of other employers have tried this method and found it helpful gives further evidence of its value. Nevertheless, the weight of experience emphasizes the limited reliability of any single type of test such as this for determining employability. Its chief value would seem to be to promote the study of the safety rules and as an interest-arouser.

6

Effective Safety Programme

The essentials of top-rate safety performance in any given establishment may be summarized as follows :

1. *There must be forceful, continuous executive leadership.*
2. *Plant and equipment must be made safe.*
3. *Supervision must be competent and intensely safety minded.*
4. *Full employee cooperation in accident prevention must be secured and maintained.*

For any continuing project at extensive as is implied in the above and necessarily also involving and influencing the work activities of the entire employed personnel, a definite planned program is necessary. Although the details will vary in different establishments, there are certain time-tried and proven activities that are found so consistently in establishments whose injury rates are of the best, that it seems safe to pronounce all of them essential to top-rate performance.

The safety program and the activities carried on under it have the purpose of (a) reducing the hazard factor (b) developing safe and adequate behaviour by every employee. A point previously made is emphasized; that in every case of work-connected injury there must be some degree of hazard (chance of injury) and unsafe or otherwise faulty behavior. But no work activities can ever be made entirely hazard free. Perfect behavior by everyone cannot be attained. Therefore, top-rate safety performance (the maximum injury elimination) can be had only by reducing the factor of hazard to the minimum, and concurrently developing employee behaviour to the maximum degree of excellence.

Finding and correcting the hazards

Activities whose major purposes is hazard elimination are :

1. *Planning*
2. *Safety in purchasing*
3. *Inspection*
4. *Job safety (or hazard) analysis*
5. *Accident investigation*

Planning for the prevention of accidents should, of course, be an intimate part of the planning and development of the entire undertaking. If this procedure is followed, a new plant or project of any kind can have so low a factor of hazard that, with reasonably good management and attention to the development of safe behaviour, human injury can be practically eliminated in its operation. However, given a plant already in operation, planning is still important because of the almost continuous changes in process, procedures and the like, and also because of the continuing modifications necessary to keep operations and equipment abreast of industrial progress. Each such change, new operation, or modification should be carefully planned to eliminate as much of the hazard factor as is possible.

A definite system of *inspection* should be set up to cover all of the plant and everything in it. Not only may hazards have been overlooked in the planning, erection, and equipment of the plant, but more important, the daily wear and tear and the changes made cause hazards to develop, which are likely, in the absence of adequate inspection, to come to light only when they yield injury. Therefore, every management should set up a system of inspection suitable to its needs.

Quantity production has been made possible only by very thorough planning of each operation and piece of equipment involved, as well as the maintenance of control adequate to insure that the work will go as planned even if the initial planning proves to be faulty, and suitable modifications must be made. This process eliminates most of the hazards and develops reliable, skilled behavior, thereby eliminating most of the injuries. However, in even our most modern, up-to-date establishments, this sort of planning and control is ordinarily extended only to the production jobs and has not been applied to such non-productive work as shipping and receiving, maintenance, repairs, and the like. These are high hazard activities, but if the safety methods of work for such jobs are worked out, the hazard points discovered, the advisable safeguards determined and provided for, and proper training provided, injuries can be eliminated as effectively from them as from quantity production work. Thus, safety men have modified the ordinary type of job analysis used for production and are applying it as *job safety* analysis to eliminate accidents in work that has not been subjected to quantity production procedures.

Both *inspection* and *job safety* analysis bring many unsafe practices to light, but that is not their chief function. The control of worker action is primarily a supervisory function. Whatever unsafe acts and practices are turned up by the three activities mentioned above should be made known to supervision promptly as a sort of extra dividend.

In spite of all that is done, some hazards will remain

overlooked or not adequately safeguarded, and some behavior faults will continue. Therefore, there will be some accidents resulting in human injury. Obviously, each of these should be investigated. *Accident investigation,* therefore, is in the nature of a post-mortem whereby the investigator seeks to discover information that will be helpful in preventing a repetition.

All of these activities will be of no avail unless the proper and fully adequate corrective action is provided for throughout. Planning that does not eliminate or reduce hazards is valueless. Inspection that does not discover conditions subject to correction or improvement is useless. Job safety analysis that does not develop better working methods and information that will be helpful in placing and training workers has been wasted. Finally, an accident investigation that results in no useful information or any recommendations for corrective action might as well not have been made.

Developing safe behavior

The techniques that have proved effective in dealing with unsafe acts are perhaps not so definite and clear-cut as those by which the hazards may be found, because they involve, for the most part, merely the adaptation of methods widely used in advertising, education, and training. An adequate program of developing and maintaining safe behavior must include the continuance of safety advertising whereby all employees are favorably conditioned to receive specific ideas and participate in specific safety activities. Along with and as a part of this advertising program must go information material whereby the employees will receive a general education in safety principles and safety measures. However, just as advertising alone, without face to face contact between salesmen and customers, will sell few goods, the advertising and educational program of itself will cause few employees to develop safe methods of work because it is only the unusual individual who will apply to his own day-by-day thinking and actions the general information and ideas that he receives through an advertising and educational program of a general nature. Therefore, all of this must be supplemented by on-the-job training in specific procedures on an individual basis. Except for vestibule or other specific training preparatory for the firing line job, the training must be given by the foreman, or under his direction.

Specific activities whose primary purpose is to develop safe and adequate behavior are :

Placement: Job safety analysis will have determined the human qualifications needed for each specific job. Proper pre-employment physical and aptitude tests and, in some cases, psychological analysis make it possible to place the job applicant in work best suited to his abilities. Haphazard placement is undoubtedly at the root of many injuries.

Training: Job analysis will have determined the safe methods of work and will have developed the information the worker needs. However, in training him for proper functioning, the detailed method of training expressed so well by the simple formula "Tell him, show him, have him do it, correct him until he has it, supervise him to see that he keeps it," expresses the fundamentals of adequate job training.

Supervision: It should be obvious that if it is true (and it certainly is) that the foreman is the key man in safety, the most careful attention should be given to the selection and training of foremen so that they can function competently in their positions of key responsibility. Therefore, a carefully worked out schedule of foreman training in safety should be a part of every safety program.

Education: A clearer distinction should be made between education and training. By education, we mean the increasing of a person's general knowledge in the fields in which he works, and in allied fields. By training, we mean the development of skill in the doing of specific tasks or types of work. Safety education should be related to the work men do and should be presented in a manner that will stimulate their thinking.

Employee Participation: Since the great majority of people learn mainly "in the doing," and since also their interest is enlisted chiefly by personal participation, the maximum in employee participation in safety activities and allied undertakings should be sought. It is possible in the well-organized and adequate safety program to assign some specific part to every employee in the organization.

Keeping the program up to the mark

Methods of appraisal of safety program requires continuous supervision and appraisal if performance is to be kept up to the mark. Careful watch must be kept on quality of performance in each of the various activities, even though appraisal may be difficult: definite standards or bench-marks are, for the most part, infeasible, and one must take into consideration the circumstances of the individual case. The important point is that the safety director or other executive having primary responsibility for the functioning of the safety program must set suitable goals and must adopt means of gauging performance in the program as a whole and in each of its various parts.

7

Occupational Safety

In the very early days of industrial legislation, it became evident that legislation by itself was not enough. The Factory Commission of 1833 made a survey of conditions in the developing textile areas, and found that earlier factory legislation had been 'almost entirely inoperative with respect to the legitimate objects contemplated by it.' It recommended the setting up of a professional inspectorate, appointed and padi by the government and responsible for enforcing the law. As a result, the Factory Act of 1833 authorised by King William IV by warrant under his sign manual to appoint during his Majesty's pleasure four persons to be Inspectors of Factories—a daring innovation at that time.

The first four 'H.M. Inspectors' so appointed were a vigorous group of men, who had to work out a new role without precedents or guide-lines. They made mistakes, but they also made a strong impact on public life; their report became vital social documents of the industrial revolution. The Hammonds summed up the importance of the inspection provision in the otherwise very limited Factory Act of 1833 in these words—'The Government had wanted to do as little as possible in the way of a Factory Act; they had done a great deal more than they intended.'

From these pioneering beginnings the British Factory Inspectorate initiated a form of government action which received international support in 1947 by I.L.O. Convention. In the newly developing countries as well as in those with a longer industrial history, we now expect to find qualified government 'labour inspectors' maintaining organised inspection of workplaces and working conditions as part of the effort to improve health and safety at work. A striking feature of these various national inspectorates is how they have come to share a common professionalism, in spite of wide differences in their origins, and in the social, political and legal systems of the countries in which they operate.

In Britain, this system developed until recently in a characteristically pragmatic and piecemeal fashion. The factory inspectors, originally concerned solely with textile factories, were given wider duties, especially after 1867, until they became responsible for inspecting factories of all kinds, building work, civil engineering and dock work. At the same time, other bodies of law, with their enforcing inspectorates, came into being to cover further areas of work and risk, such as mining, railways, explosive, petroleum and, much later, agriculture, offices, retailing and nuclear installations.

After the second World War, it became evident that this piecemeal approach was inadequate for the speed and scope of technological developments, and to meet growing social awareness. In 1970, the Robens Committee was appointed with wide terms of reference to review provisions made for the health and safety of persons in all kinds of employment and for protecting the public against hazards from industrial and commercial activities. The Report of the Committee, became the basis of the health and Safety at Work, etc., Act 1974, which cam substantially into force on 1 April 1975.

In addition to its new legal provisions this Act makes sweeping changes in government organisation, including arrangements for inspection. At the time of writing, these organisational changes are not yet complete, but the present period of change provides opportunity for taking stock—for looking at past experience and at hopes prospects for the future. For reasons of space, we shall confine ourselves almost exclusively to the experience of factory inspectors, but other inspectors should not be forgotten. These each have their own bodies of experience and will also be involved in the change which are in hand.

The first duty of factory inspectors was to enforce the law; but from 1833 onwards, there has been a continuing debate as to how the word 'enforce' is to be understood. Should inspectors simply look for breaches of the law, and prosecute when they find them? Or should they give their main efforts to advice and persuasion, having recourse to the courts only as a last resort? On the whole, the British Factory Inspectorate has followed the latter line'; it has measured its success not by the number of convictions secured but by how far the substantial aims to the law are achieved.

Inspectors have come to accept it as part of their duty not only to explain what the law says, but also to advise as to how its aims can be best achieved. As a result, the Inspectorate now provides a technical advisory service about health, safety and welfare at work. It headquarters office has become a clearing house for information. It publishes, through H.M. Stationary Office, a wide range of advisory material for the use of employers and employees. It operates an Industrial Health and Safety Centre at Horseferry Road, London. Inspectors are heavily in demand as a technical lectures for societies and institutions concerned with occupational health and safety. More important, though perhaps less obvious, inspectors during their ordinary work receive countless queries with they have to try to answer out of their own experience or from the wider resources of the Inspectorate.

Underlying all this is a continuous responsibility to be alert for anything which may affect the health or safety of employed persons—to be, in effect, a skilled watchdog on their behalf. The word 'skilled' is used advisedly. One of the most distinctive skills of an ordinary inspector in the field is the ability to recognise a risk or matter needing attention, often in an unfamiliar form and an unexpected place. This is an essentially detective or diagnostic skill, which is quite different from that of applying detailed regulations.

It would be rash to claim that factory inspectors, either individually or as an organised service, have always performed these functions as well as they should. Inspectors are but human, and the Inspectorate has not always measured up to the demands made upon it. However, a study of the way in which labour inspections has developed in many countries gives strong ground for believing that it success depends upon a combination of these three complementary elements—of effective legal *enforcement* of sound technical *advice,* and of skilled *watchfullness.*

These three elements have to be kept in balance. The primary responsibility for preventing occupational accidents and disease 'lies with those who create the risks and those who work with them.' The wrong sort of free advisory service could have the result of encouraging industry to unload on to government the task of finding answers to all the health and safety problems which industry itself has created—which would be not only wasteful, but damaging. Even to-day there are still too many managements who are content to leave it to the inspector' to tell them what to do about safety, without taking any initiative themselves. Advice needs to be linked with sanctions which can be used, when necessary, to bring home to managements and employees their direct responsibility for tackling their own health and safety problems. Once that responsibility is recognise, an adequate inspectorate can do much 'to help industry to help itself' and so can contribute to the broader effort for health and safety at work'.

The development of the work of factory inspectors over the past 142 years has therefore resulted in a wide expansion of their areas of professional concern. They are still responsible for regulating hours of work, but in addition have had to develop specialised expertise in three broad areas—in accident prevention, in the prevention of occupational disease, and in matters of welfare and of the general working environment.

Factory inspectors had at first no direct responsibility for safety. They were soon aware, however, of the dangers of unprotected machinery in textile mills, and of accidents which occurred; and they reported these things to the Home Secretary. The first amending Act, in 1844, contained specific safety provisions. Inspectors became increasingly involved in discussion on safety standards—discussion which led to some heated controversies with employers and their organisations. This early example illustrates the two-way relationship between inspection and legislation which has characterised the whole process. The inspectors were not content to be simply neutral enforcing officers; they saw it as part of their professional duty to inform and to stimulate legislation to deal with the practical conditions they discovered in their work. From this beginning, occupational safety has become one of the main concerns of inspectors.

The basis of sound accident prevention must be experience of previous accidents. For this purpose, any accident to an employee in a place subject to the Factories Act has to be reported if it causes more than three days lost time. These reports are used by the Inspectorate for statistical studies and for selective investigation. It should be emphasised that inspectors are not directly concerned with compensation or civil liability; their investigations are directed solely to enforcing safety law, and to gaining experience for preventing accidents.

Accidents are of many kinds. Some can be prevented by sound regulations properly observed; others can hardly be prevented by the most elaborate legislation. Different kinds of accidents have deferring 'severity potentials'— that is, certain types, though not necessarily causing severe injury in every case, are more likely than average to inflict severe injury. In factories, three broad groups of accidents have relatively high severity potentials:

(a) accidents from power-driven machinery, including mechanical lifting and handling;

(b) the 'technical' hazards of fire, explosion, gassing and electricity;

(c) accidents due to persons and articles falling from above ground level.

Accidents of these three types causes about one quarter of the lost time injuries in factories but they produce about a half of the severe injuries and 90 per cent of fatalities. The continuing concern of inspectors with machinery safety has a sound basis in experience, which is sometimes obscured by using total accidents figures without taking account of severity.

The approach of inspectors has therefore been selective. They have not felt themselves to be concerned equally with preventing every type of accident which may conceivably happen; they have concentrated deliberately on a limited sector—on those things which may cause the graver and more insides risks, and which may be more effectively controlled by legislation. To make this distinction is not to ignore accidents of other sorts—e.g., from hand tools, manual handling and falls on the level. These have, however, to be tackled in other ways, and may not involve inspectors so directly.

Methods of approach need reassessment as circumstances change. Traditionally, inspectors have worked mainly by periodic surprise visits to premises, a method which concentrates attention on things which can be checked visually during a short visit. They have tended to be chiefly interested in the state of the buildings and hardware. Is this approach still appropriate to-day? Much of our modern and sophisticated plant presents few obvious risks during routine production when all is going well, but may cause serious hazards on occasions—when loading, cleaning or from some breakdown in the process. Only too often, these hazards receive attention only after there has been a major accident or disaster. Safety standards need to be worked out between technical specialists, mid-management and operatives, taking into account the whole cycle of production, and possible emergencies and deviations. These are similar developments point to the need to supplement traditional surprise visits, by methods of inspection which can probe more deeply into techniques, processes and systems of work, and which can involve higher technical management, especially at planning and design stage. How this is to be organised with limiting inspecting staff, operating in a wide and diversified field, is one of the problems of the future.

Fire hazards deserve special note, as they are two distinct types:

(a) from semi-explosive process fires, which may involve persons in flames in a few seconds.

(b) from persons being trapped by smoke and fire spread after a building has caught fire.

Factory inspectors have been closely concerned with risks of the first type, which are almost certainly an increasing risk today, with the widespread use of petrochemical and other organic compounds, many of which are highly flammable. Risks of the second type are similar to those in buildings, of all sorts, and are the primary concern of the County Fire Authorities, who are normally responsible for certifying safe means of escape and other precautions. Changes introduced by the Health and Safety at Work Act are likely to simplify this division of responsibility although there will still be need for collaboration between factory inspectors and fire officers.

Occupational diseases

We have known for a very long time that certain diseases have been linked with certain occupations—names like 'potters' 'rot' and 'printers' colic' bear witness to this. These recognisable occupational diseases were mainly due to work-people absorbing cumulative poisons by breathing dust fumes. During the early year of the present century, the Factory Inspectorate were much concerned with identifying and controlling the use of a fairly limited range of 'industrial poisons' known to cause such diseases. These poisons included lead compounds, white phosphorus, silicious dusts, and chromic acid. They were mainly encountered at that time in certain 'dangerous trades', which were made subject to special regulations—such as those covering potteries, chrome plating, asbestos processes, grinding of metals and vitreous enameling. During this period, there was a spectacular reduction in the incidence of some of these diseases—for example, from 1990 to 1938, the number of reported cases of industrial lead poisoning fell from over 1000 per year to under a hundred; during the same period, phosphorus poisoning and industrial arsenical poisoning were virtually eliminated. These successes, when contrasted with the slow changes in accident figures, sometimes created a sense of complacency.

More recently, and especially since about 1950, the subject has opened up on a far wider front. New synthetic materials are increasing coming into use, not merely in the previous dangerous trades, but in work of all sorts—as solvents, adhesives, cleansing materials, coating agents, sterilisers, etc. Some of these are quite safe, but others may create new health hazards in unexpected places. We have come to realise that some materials and conditions of work may increase liability to disease which are not exclusively occupational in character—such as bronchitis, dermatitis, allergic conditions and some cancers. The public generally are becoming increasingly aware of problems of health and disease. Consequently, many workpeople are puzzled and apprehensive as to whether their work may be affecting their health.

These developments have coincided with large changes in the health services, both on the curative and on the prevention sides. During this process, there has been widespread debate on how the health services and medical expertise should be related to people at work and to industrial activities, and as to the role of government in this relationship. This debate still continues. Four elements in the relationship have been of particular concern to factory inspectors in dealing with occupational disease:

(1) The first relates to the role of *medical practitioners* in this work. Prior to 1972, the Factory Inspectorate had a small Medical Branch, comprising inspectors with medical qualification, and also made use of Appointed Factory Doctors who were mostly part-

time and had limited duties under the Factories Act. Since 1972, these have been merged into the Employment Medical Advisory Service, distinct from the Factory Inspectorate, but maintaining close liaison with it. On the non-governmental side, many firms employ Works Doctors or Company Medical Officers of various types. The Robens Committee estimated that about 600 doctors were then employed full-time and possibly 2000 part-time by private and nationalised industry, though it was plain that the duties of these doctors differed widely in different undertakings.

(2) Sound preventive work depends on knowledge of cause and effect, and this in turn depends on *medical research*. Fundamental research on the effects of organised conditions and materials on the human body is essentially a part of such work in areas of special urgency and to keep liaison with results of research, both nationally and internationally.

(3) *Occupational hygiene* is a modern specialisation concerned with assessing and controlling, hazards from atmospheric contamination, skin absorption, radiation, noise, etc. Standards depend on results of medical knowledge but hygienists need not be medically qualified, and normally have qualifications in physics and chemistry, including techniques of atmospheric analysis. Tables of threshold limit values are available, giving quantified indication of the degree and kind of hazards associated with a very wide range of materials used at work. The informed and intelligent use of these data is an essential part of the skill of an occupational hygienist. The Factory Inspectorate set up an occupational hygiene unit in 1966, which has since been much developed. Hygienists are

employed by some larger firms, and units are attached to some universities and other bodies.

(4) A special problem of the Factory Inspectorate is the *primary inspection* of areas where occupational health risks are unlikely, but may conceivably occur. In the past, primary inspection of occupational health hazards has been based on inspectors' knowledge of the various trades, assessing particular risks by visual inspection, with the possibility of calling in specialist help in urgent cases. To-day, health hazards are far more widely dispersed; they are not necessarily linked with particular trades, nor even confined to industry. It is hard to ascertain the absence of risk simply 'by sniff and by guess'; yet it would be virtually impossible to try to apply the whole range of sophisticated occupational hygiene techniques universally in very workplace. Techniques of detection and of rough assessment are therefore needed, and some are being developed, to help to identify areas of potential risk, which may need more thorough investigation subsequently.

These aspects of the work of factory inspectors are developing rapidly, and are likely to be the subject of increasing public concern.

Welfare conditions

The Factories Act requires suitable welfare arrangements and a healthy and comfortable working environment. Most of these requirements are straight-forward and non-controversial, but they sometimes receive less attention than they deserve, perhaps because defects do not make themselves evident in accident figures or in cases of recognisable occupational disease. Yet, for most people most of the time, discomfort at work matters more than what may seem a remote risk of accident or disease.

Factory inspectors are only too aware of much needless discomfort at work, not only in factories but also in offices and commercial premises. Many work-room are uncontrollably too cold or hot for parts of the year. Ventilation in parts of a room may mean discomfort in other parts. Some of our newer buildings are among the worst offenders in these respects. Unfortunately, inspectors normally discover uncomfortable conditions only when buildings are complete and when remedies will be makeshift and costly. They develop some skill in trying to make intolerable conditions tolerable; but they have little opportunity to concern themselves with these things at design stage. This subject may come into greater prominence in the future.

The regulation of hours of work has historically the first responsibility of factory inspectors, and is still one of their duties. The Factories Act restricts the hours of employment of young persons and of women, but not of men over 18. The form of the law results in sharp differences between restrictions applying to factory work and to other comparable employments. This subject was not within the scope of the Robens Committee, and is likely to receive further consideration along with the wider question of the protection of children and young persons in industrial and non-industrial employment generally.

We have so far been looking, in very broad outline, at some of the experience of the British Factory Inspectorate up to the present time. What of the future, in view of the large changes which are now taking place? Doubtless much will continue as before; but there are some points where significant developments are in prospect. All that can be attempted here is to pick out a few of these, recognising that it is far too early to make any reliable forecast as to how they will work out.

The new administrative machinery set up by the Health and Safety at Work Act has been well publicised and will be familiar to most readers. The health and Safety Commission is responsible for general policy, including the initiation of research and the preparation of regulations and codes of practice. The Health and Safety Executive is the operational arm, which will deal with individual employers and workplaces. The staff of the Executive includes certain inspectorates which were formerly attached to various government departments—i.e. Inspectors of Factories, Mines and Quarries, Pipelines, Nuclear Installations, Alkali and Clean Air and Explosives. It includes the Employment Medical Advisory Service and scientific support services such as the Safety in Mines Research Establishment.

The Factory Inspectorate therefore becomes one of the component inspectorate within the Health and Safety Executives. At the present time, these inspectorates maintain their distinctive functions and organisations, although it is plainly intended that they will work together more closely. The local District structure of the Factory Inspectorate is being reorganised into larger areas, as recommended in the Robens Report.

Unless otherwise provided, enforcement is by inspectors attached to the Executives, but there are powers to allocate enforcement duties by regulations to other bodies, including local authorities. It is apparently intended to allocate inspection of some types of 'non-industrial employment' to District Councils, but no regulations have been made.

Safety regulations

The Health and Safety at work Act does not contain a new codes of detailed safety provisions; instead it sets up an administrative organisation for continuously generating and revising detailed codes as needed. This feature is based on the behalf that, with the rate of technical change, detailed safety provisions are out of place in an Act of Parliament. At present 'existing statutory provisions' are continued in force, the Commission having responsibility to initiate revision by regulations as changes are needed.

Regulation making under the Factories Act has often a lengthy process, especially where a number of interests were involved. The Commission has a wide field, covering almost the whole employed population. Many matters with which it is concerned will impinge on the work of various government departments and trade interests. Increasingly, national safety standards need to be harmonised by means of international consultation. On the face of it, therefore, the drafting and revising of regulations and odes of practical likely to prove a very heavy and continuing load of work for the Commission and its staff.

Involvement of employees

The factories Act exists to protect employed persons, but it has given virtually no place to employees or their organisations in its local working. The statutory recognition of 'employees safety representatives' in the Health and Safety at Work Act is therefore a very important innovation. This follows broadly similar arrangements in the Mines and Quarries Act, 1954, for the rather special conditions of coal-mining. Similar arrangements exist in Swedish law.

The primary aim of these provisions is to encourage direct consultation between employers and employees as to local safety arrangements. There are provisions for inspectors to provide relevant information. This development is of great potential and may have a strong impact on safety methods—and, incidentally, on the work of inspectors. The vital question is how trade unions, and employers generally will use the opportunities it creates.

Most previous safety legislation has been divided sharply between legislation to protect people at work and that to protect the public at large. Normally, the two areas have been covered by separate law, enforced by different authorities. The Robens Committee recommended a reorientation of approach; it proposed that legislation and enforcement be unified to protect all persons, whether employed or not, from hazards arising in workplaces or from working processes. The responsibilities of the Commission and Executive have been drawn accordingly.

One aspect of this subject which received close attention was the need to protect the public, as well as employees, from the very large-scale hazards which sometimes accompany modern industrial operations. Recent events have underlined this danger, and it became one of the first concerns of the Commission after its appointment.

Another aspect which has so far had less attention is the effect of the new legislation in workplaces where a minority of employed persons are involved along with a greater number who are not employees. Typical examples are schools, colleges and hospitals. Any attempt to consider employee safety in these places, apart from the safety of school children, students or patients would be quite unrealistic. The only practical approach seems to be to deal comprehensively with the safety of the workplace and its activities as a whole. This will have a substantial effect on the responsibilities of the Executive. Somewhat similar considerations may arise in some retail stores and in places of entertainment.

One of the main features of the new legislation is its comprehensiveness covering all employment. This brings

8 million more persons within the scope of inspection, as well as covering aspects of public safety. Perhaps more significant, the scope is based on employment and not on premises. Inspection under most earlier legislation could be directed to cover all premises listed as subject to the appropriate Act; the present legislation has no such boundary. Practically all buildings, apart from dwelling-houses, are work-pieces; and in addition much work is done away from fixed workplaces. Even allowing for division of duties between the Executive and other authorities, the need will remain to devise a realistic and comprehensive system of inspection to cover this wide diversity of work. Inspection will have to be directed not only towards examining workplaces, but to much greater extent towards checking systems of work.

As we have seen, the various inspectors became involved in assembling and providing technical advice by pressure of events rather than by conscious decision. The Health and Safety Commission has been set up from the start with explicit powers and duties to initiate research and investigation, and to circulate and disseminate technical information on matters of occupational health safety. Trade and academic bodies will doubtless carry out much of the actual research, but the Commission will be in a position to keep in touch with results, and to be the official focal point for information on these subjects. Because of its comprehensive responsibility, the Commission will be in a far stronger position to fulfill this role than were the separate headquarter organisations of the various inspectorates in the past. This therefore is likely to be an important area of development.

In some ways, the problems of disseminating and applying technical information are even greater than those of collecting it. In this context, it needs to be realised that the inspection of areas where 'technical' risks are infrequent but occur occasionally often makes greater demands on the technical knowledge of the inspector than does the inspection of work where technical hazards are more obvious and therefore more familiar to managements. The intention seems to be that local 'Area' offices of the Executive should be developed as local resource centres. A special problem will be to maintain practical liaison between the Executive and Local Authority officers who may be allocated enforcement duties for certain types of employment. For this purpose, the location of Area offices will be important.

8
Mechanical Safety

A general acceptance of the importance of mechanical safety can only be achieved if everyone in the organisation is given training in the principles involved. On the engineering side safety consciousness must be engendered in the design department, emphasised in the installation or erection department, and continually demonstrated in the maintenance department. The maintenance department also has a responsibility to feed back safety experience to the design department.

The effectiveness of safety measures in the production department is increased if the line production manager is responsible for safety there. He can then lay down procedures for his operators to carry out routine checks on safety devices and immediately report any failures or abnormalities in their operation.

The proper layout of machines is an obvious starting point for ensuring safety in the machine shop. Adequate space between machines and between the machines and walls must be provided taking due account of the type of work to be handled. Although this statement seems to be elementary it is nevertheless not long ago that a case was reported in one of the safety journals in which an apprentice was trapped between a wall and traversing table of a milling machine while being instructed in its use by a skilled tradesman.

On a number of machines the traversing handles

rotate under power whilst the machine is operating, and this can be hazard even if regulation overalls are worn. Disked wheels instead of handles are useful in avoiding this hazard.

Controls on machines are sometimes placed in unsafe positions. A typical example is a case in which a lathe operator used a bar as a lever to remove the face plate at the conclusion of a job. The control lever for stopping the lathe was near the headstock and the man's body accidentally pressed it, causing the lathe to rotate and trapping his hand between the bar and the machine framework. The control lever should have been designed so that it had to be pulled towards the operator rather than pushed away from him to start the machine. In any case it should have been repositioned in a safer place.

A Similar point arises in connection with electrical start buttons on machines. To avoid any confusion, one *start* push-button only should be provided on any machine and should be shrouded so that if any person or object fell against it the machine would not start inadvertently. Conversely, because of the need to make the *stop* push-buttons easily accessible for quickly stopping a machine in an emergency, such buttons should have large exposed mushroom heads. The colours of push-buttons should be in accordance with British Standards non-resetting type. Regular cleaning of control buttons is essential so that not only do the colours remain clearly visible but also to ensure that the movements are not impeded by layers of greases or dirt. Guarding of the work on milling machines in a jobbing workshop can be a problem, but various effective adjustable types of guard are now available.

Drilling machines can also present problems. As opposed to the telescopic guard which fits over the chuck and twist drill, a device comprising a vertical trip bar located close to the drill and suspended from a snap-action changeover switch has advantages as far as visibility and general accessibility are concerned. This device is usually used in connection with reverse plugging braking of the drill motor, and any displacement of the trip bar by more than a few degrees will actuate the safety circuit. The switch is not self-resetting so that the machine does not restart when the trip bar is restored to its normal position.

Safety in the factory

Although care is necessary in guarding machines in the machine shop the situation there is helped by the fact that the operators are generally skilled craftsmen and therefore aware of the hazards of the equipment which they are using. In the factory department the process operator may be put more at risk by hurrying to meet production schedules. It is therefore necessary to take even more care in these situations to provide adequate guarding which will not easily defeated by maloperation.

A great variety of devices is employed but most of the important principles are illustrated in the two following examples of protection of an automatic soap-wrapping machine and a paper-cutting guillotine.

The wrapping machine wraps soap tablets which are fed in on the left-hand side of the picture. The machine is fitted on four sides with an open-top welded mesh guard. The 'high wall' feature makes access to moving parts extremely difficult and these can be considered to be safe by position. With the exception of the front hinged guard doors, all guards are fixed and can only be removed with the use of a spanner. Access to the machine for the purpose of effecting or removing a blockage is attained only *via* the two front hinged doors. These doors can only be opened after first raising the guard rail, initial movement of which breaks a magnetic switch and the machine is immediately stopped. The magnetic switch is preferred to other types because it is less easy to defeat normal operation.

The welded mesh guard depicted in this illustration has the advantage that it affords the operator a reasonably good view of the interior of the machine without producing any reflections. In some cases, however, where total enclosure is necessary, e.g., to protect against dust, a transparent plastic guard may be appropriate in spite of the fact that it does produce some reflection. Care should be taken to use a material which is not easily flammable. The two extension pieces fitted to the side guard protect the belt terminal pulleys and prevent the operator from being 'nipped' between the belt and pulley.

Complementary to conventional mechanical guarding, some modern machines use a sophisticated system of light beams impinging on photoelectric cells for guarding areas where a high degree of visibility or accessibility is required. On breaking the beam the machine stops. With the guillotine, the stopping time is just over representing a vertical movement of the knife of 0.14 in. On the same machine there is a requirement for 'hand cranking' for knife adjustment purposes. The machine is equipped with a large flywheel which requires some min to reach standstill after switching off, and it is essential that the hand-cranking operation be performed with the flywheel at standstill. A process timer is inserted in the machine control system to ensure that the hand-cranking circuit cannot be energised until after the flywheel has ceased to rotate.

Important as it is to provide a high standard of guarding on machines it must also be emphasised that all operators should be adequately trained in the operation of machines on which they work. Systematic training schemes in which the departmental supervisor participates are of value to make sure that this training is kept up to date.

Electrical tools

Portable electrical equipment

Items of portable hand-held electrical equipment such as drills, sanders, and inspection plight are of great help in increasing factory productivity but care must be taken to ensure the use of correct current rating of cable and h.r.c. fuse, and that adequate inspection and maintenance is provided. The hazards of this type of equipment are greater than those obtaining with fixed equipment because the supply is changed from a permanent installation to a temporary one by the use of flexible cables and plugs and sockets.

To minimise these hazards it is common practice to use some form of reduced voltage supply and two typical systems are worthy of mention. In the first, transformers are permanently installed in the plant with outputs of either 110 V or 50 V a.c. at 50 HZ, the secondary being centre tapped and solidly connected to earth thus reducing the shock risk to 55 or 25 V respectively. The second employs special portable transformers of similar outputs connected on the primary side to appropriately positioned mains voltage socket outlets.

Each system has its advantages. The first, that no flexible connection carries a voltage of more than 55 V to earth, and that no heavy transformers have to be carried about together with the tools. In the second, the total capital cost of the system is less but it must be borne in mind that some flexible cables are live at mains voltage to earth.

To prevent any risk of plugging a low-voltage tool into a mains voltage supply a different type of socket-outlet be used.

When using hand-held tools the operator may be subjected to one or more of the following four hazards:

(a) working in contact with earthed metal,

(b) working in an inaccessible position,

(c) working in hot or damp conditions

(d) working at a height above floor level.

In any system using Class I tools as defined in B.S. 2769, socket outlets situated in areas where three or more of these hazards are present should be regarded as high risk and fitted with earth leakage protection, so that in the event of an earth fault occurring the supply automatically disconnected. In places where two of hazards exist, the situation can be considered on its own merits to determine whether or not an earth leakage protection should be provided. If only one hazard exists the use of low voltage equipment coupled with a regular inspection procedure of the type outlined in the following paragraphs is considered adequate without the use of earth leakage protection.

The introduction of all-insulated and double-insulted tools is likely to do away with the need for earth leakage protection, but many installations of the type described will continue in use for some time. Whatever type of steps are taken to achieve safety, regular inspection of all portable equipment, including tools, lamps, or transformers, is essential and the following simple arrangements are recommended.

All equipment should be kept in a central store where there are also facilities for testing. Each item should have a registered number and record card and be issued to a user department only against a duly authorised requisition. Requisitions should be valid for 2 weeks, after which time the equipment must be returned for test unless it has been returned earlier on completion of use.

To ensure that all equipment not returned in this time is followed up, a simple 14-pattern filing cabinet may be used. All record cards of equipment issued on a given day will then be filed together with the question in one section of the cabinet, marked with a date of 14 days in advance of the issue date. Hence on any day the cards in the container marked with that date will show the equipment still out on loan and due for test. The storekeeper sill send out a request for the return of the equipment and it this should produce no result in 3 days it will be followed with an 'urgent' form printed in red and prohibiting further use of the equipment. Should this also produce no result the storekeeper will send a man to collect the equipment from the user department. This procedure has proved to be necessary for a large company and experience has shown that only 10 percent of initial reminders and 1 per cent of 'follow-up' notes need to be sent. It could of course be modified to suit the smaller user.

When equipment is received back in the tore after use it should be placed with the record card in a 'for inspection and test' section. The test procedure should include visual inspection of the equipment, cable, and plug, for external damage. For Class I equipment these tests should also include a heavy current resistance test between the earthed metal of the plug and the metal body of the equipment, and an insulation test between the live pins of the plug and its earthed metal. In carrying out the last test it must be remembered that the switch on the portable equipment should be in the 'on' position. For other classes of equipment of the appropriate tests are made.

The results should be entered on the record card

together with a note of any repairs carried out, and the card initialled by the electrician carrying out the work.

Mobile electrical equipment

There is often equipment in factories which is not permanently wired but which by virtue of its size or position has to be inspected on site rather than in the test room. Voltages of this type of equipment should be kept as low as practicable but because of the power required may involve the use of a two- or three-phase supply. Where mains voltage equipment is essential the cable feeding it should be fitted with duplicate earth paths, one of which be provided open all this type of equipment.

The frequency of inspection of the equipment will vary with its type, the situation in which it is used, and the frequency of use. The factory electrical engineer should decide the inspection intervals in the light of these factors, but they should never exceed 3 months.

Each item should have a record card and the cards be filed in a system which providers reminders when inspectors are due. The tests carried out will generally be similar to those for portable equipment, but in this case the continuity of each of the duplicate earth paths in the cables must also be tested.

Electrical control gear

The manufacturers of electrical control gear subject all new designs to more stringent conditions than are met in actual service, before putting them into production. Subsequently they test all production equipment before dispatch to the purchasers. If these precautions are supplemented by regular testing after installation the user can be assured of safe and reliable operation. He should also ensure that operators are given training in the correct method of using the equipment.

A simple example is the use of 'sequence' starting, in which the pressing of one start push-button may initiate the operation of not one but several conveyors. To ensure safety during cleaning and general maintenance, isolating switches should be locked in the 'off' position and their keys retained by a responsible person until work is finished. This precaution should also be supplemented by hanging a notice on the switch worded *Caution, do not start; man working on equipment.*

Where the isolating switches are associated with motors they should be fitted with a fourth pole, isolating the control circuit. This will enable that if a remote start push-button is inadvertently pressed whilst the switch is open, the motor will not restart when it is closed.

In sequence schemes there may be live contacts in the isolating switch associated with the motor even though it is in the 'off' position. A prominent notice to this effect should be placed on the isolating switch cover as a reminder to the maintenance electrician when he removes it for inspection purposes.

The designers of fuse gear and switchgear also pay considerable attention to the provision of safety interlock stop prevent unauthorised tampering. For example, on combinations of fuses and switches, interlocks are provided so that firstly the cover cannot be operated with the cover open. Fuse-carriers and fuse-bases are also designed so that live metal cannot be touched whilst withdrawing or replacing the fuse-carrier.

The placing of electrical equipment is important, and positions beneath water or stream pipes must be avoided. Where it is impossible to avoid such positions adequate screen should be provided to protect the electrical gear because any protective enclosure is vulnerable when doors are opened for maintenance purposes.

To supplement the continuing improvements in writing of national standards and the subsequent care taken by the manufacturing industry, the user must play his part in ensuring safety throughout the life of the equipment. Correct training and strict supervision are therefore essential for all electricians responsible for maintenance work on electrical control gear.

9

Industrial Safety

This chapter will tell in very brief form how the safety movement in American industry developed, and will also call attention to certain things in the manner of its development that will add to an understanding of the situation as it stands after a half century of effort by at first hundreds, then thousands, then tens of thousands of devoted and splendidly motivated participants. Much that is faulty or lacking in the safety movement today is due, in large part at least, to mistakes made in the formative years, mistakes that arose largely out of bitterness carried over from the long years of struggle that finally brought corrective action by state governments and an organized safety movement by, and in, private industry.

As pointed out in the preceding chapter, accidental injuries have always been a familiar part of life and living and working. Since obviously unsafe behavior was involved in nearly every case of such injury, the injury was regarded as primarily the accident victim's own fault. This did not matter much in the handicraft era. Home workshops were the rule; such plants as there were were powered by waterwheels, if at all. Injury rates could not have been high or many of the injuries serious, so when an injury did occur, it was taken as a matter of course. The employer felt no responsibility for it nor did his employees expect him to.

The advent of the steam engine, followed by the electric motor and the tremendous increase in the use of power driven machinery that it made possible, soon brought an increasing stream of serious and fatal injuries. This soon brought a change in the worker's attitude. It was easy to see that when a workman was killed or injured by a hazardous condition that could obviously have been safeguarded, or eliminated, the employer was at least partly at fault. This change in thinking was sped by the shocking nature of many of these occurrences; workmen whirled to death when their clothing was caught by projecting set screws on line shafting; crushed flat between belt and pulley; flesh eaten away upon falling into an unprotected floor-level acid vat; chewed up inch by inch when caught in massive gears or screw conveyers, etc.

The great industrial expansion, particularly of heavy, high hazard industry, that followed the depression of the 70's, accelerated the upward trend of serious and fatal injuries. The newspapers became interested and tended more and more to print the gory details of the more serious cases. Public interest grew. Organized labor, though weak in those days, used every means at its command to develop public support for its demands for corrective action.

Labour fought for two things: the guarding of hazardous machinery and correction of other serious hazards, and, recompense for the accident victims and their dependents, particularly in cases of serious permanent disablement or death. Leading clergymen and other humanitarian minded leaders joined in the struggle, and, gradually, public demand for correction grew.

The first law requiring the guarding of hazardous machinery was enacted in Massachusetts in 1877 in response to widespread indignation and concern over an especially sympathy-arousing type of injury-the fingers of young girls were being cut off or mangled by the gears of spinning machines in textile plants. The girls had to work with their fingers very close to the in-running sides of these gears and the toll of fingers was heavy. In spite of this, it took many years of agitation to get this law passed. How many young fingers and mangled hands it cost will never be known; such records were not kept until workmen's compensation legislation made them necessary, but there can be no doubt that over the long years before the guarding was installed the total number of such accidents ran into very large figures. Gradually other states followed with guarding laws. By 1900 most of the heavily industrialized states had at least some form of safeguarding legislation with factory inspection to enforce it.

Labour's other demand, compensation for the accident victims, was gained only after a much longer and even harder struggle. Employer resistance was augmented by the fact that this demand became identified with the larger struggle for higher wages, shorter hours, and better working conditions. Unrestrained immigration kept wages at bare subsistence levels. Working conditions were deplorable. Very few plants paid any attention at all to the health and safety of the workers. Ventilation received no attention whatever. Light came usually only from windows and these were often small. Sanitation was minimal. The struggle was long and bitter, largely because the realization that employers would profit by having well-paid, contented workers was slow in coming.

The passage of legislation requiring employers to provide safeguards against certain specified hazards furnished at least some legal basis for the thesis, now thoroughly established by both law and custom, that the employer is responsible for all injuries to his employees while at their work for him. Many employers early in our industrial development accepted this view to the extent of assuming the costs of medical treatment for injured employees and the burial expenses of those killed by accidents. Some provision was often made for the widow, perhaps as a domestic in the home of the employer or through a rent-free cottage. Frequently the employer had a collection taken up for a widow or a permanently disabled victim to which he contributed according to the generosity of his spirit.

The utter inadequacy of such relief measures brought about the practice of suing for damages under common law. Some of these suits were successful, but, as court decisions multiplied and lawyers retained by the employers developed the technique of defending them, it became increasingly difficult to obtain awards. The courts came to recognize three common-law defenses. The first was "contributory negligence," namely, that the4 worker injured had by some action or lack of action contributed to the accident. This was an extremely difficult defense to over come because faulty behavior in some degree is a contributory factor in nearly every case. The second defense, the theory of "the assumption of risk," held that when a worker accepted employment he knew or should have known the risks involved in the work and assumed them. To overcome this defense, it was usually necessary to show that the hazard was out of the ordinary for the employment in question or that the employer was grossly negligent.

Under this system a vicious racket known as "ambulance chasing" developed. Lawyers following this practice would get to an accident victim (or his heir in case of a fatality) as quickly as possible and get his signature on a retainer agreement. The lawyer would drive as hard a bargain as he could but would always take care to get a substantial share of the award, if any. Usually his share plus expenses left little or nothing for the accident victim. These lawyers soon discovered that, while in most cases they could not overcome the common-law defenses and win an award for the accident victim, they could frequently get a small settlement from the employer by threatening to take the case to court. Seldom, however, did the unfortunate client get more than a small fraction of any such settlement. Ambulance chasers were also retained by many employers to induce the accident victim to accept a small payment and sign a release instead of going to court. Such employers sometimes went to great lengths to insure that such releases would be obtained. It is obvious that under such conditions the accident victims fare badly indeed.

Employer liability laws

The intent of this type of legislation was to make it easier for the accident victim to obtain an award when employer negligence could be shown. However, such legislation proved of little value because of the difficulty of proving the employer negligent. Also, it left the ambulance chaser undisturbed. So labor and its supporters turned to a type of legislation that had been developed under Bismarck in Germany in 1885 and which had soon spread across most of Europe and to England, namely, workmen's compensation legislation.

Workmen's compensation laws

this type of law eliminates the question of fault. Its purpose is, roughly, "to provide for the compensation of all injuries arising out of, or in connection with, employment." It requires the employer to pay the injured worker's medical and hospital expenses plus compensation which will furnish to him and his dependents, if any, at least a minimum subsistence during his period of disability. Also, under proper administration the worker who has a legitimate claim need not be put to any expense in order to secure the compensation due him.

The first such compensation law in this country was enacted by Congress in 1908, but the benefits were very meager and they were limited to certain special classes of federal workers. Several states passed laws of this type about this time but they were held unconstitutional. Finally, in 1911, New Jersey passed a law that was upheld. Other states rapidly followed this lead; seven in 1911, three in 1912, eleven in 1913, two in 1914, and ten in 1915. In 1948 Mississippi, the 48th state to act, passed a workmen's compensation law. The territories of Alaska and Hawaii had passed such laws in 1915. In 1919 employees of the District of Columbia government were covered by such a law. In 19128 the coverage was extended to private industry in the District.

No state law covers all its employed persons, however. Some exclude a very substantial proportion of them. Domestic service is not covered in any state, nor, with few exceptions, are any farm workers. Most laws exclude very small employers and a few exclude minor branches of industry that are characterized by small workforces; for example, logging is excluded in some southern states.

The various laws differ in other ways also, but, in addition to eliminating the factor of fault, all of them:

1. Provide for at least a substantial part of the medical expense involved in each case of injury.
2. Establish a definite method of computing the compensation to be paid an injured workman, tying the amount of the payment to the wages of the injured workman and setting a minimum intended to approximate a subsistence income.

3. Provide that in cases of total permanent disability or death, benefits shall continue at least during a period of readjustment. The more liberal acts provide benefits during the entire period of disability or, in case of death, during the entire period of dependency of the widow and children.

By making work injuries immediately and inescapably expensive to employers, workmen's compensation laws have done more to promote their interest in safety than all other influences put together. As the worker's knowledge of his rights under these laws spread, claims increased rapidly in number and the cost to the employers grew to such substantial figures, particularly in large, high injury plants, that many of them initiated extensive programs of hazard elimination. They usually were very expensive because of the heavy cost of guarding the machinery, particularly the power transmission machinery, but it soon became clear that the saving of a few deaths or serious permanent disabilities would pay for a lot of guards. A few socially minded employers had begun the correction of obviously serious hazards long before the passage of workmen's compensation legislation, but the great majority had done little or nothing. Incidentally, the cost of guarding extensive systems of mechanical power transmission was a major factor in the rapid development and adoption of direct motor drives for the individual machines.

The first continuing plant safety program of record was started in the Joliet works of the Illinois Steel Company in 1892 by the formation of a committee of plant executives with authority to act. Their first action was to order the inspection and testing of all flywheels in the plant because of a disastrous flywheel explosion. Soon a full-time safety director was appointed and safety thus became a recognized part of plant operation. One by one other plants in steel and other high injury rate industries took similar action, but it wasn't until enough states had passed compensation laws to make it clear that they would become general, that the possibility of holding costs down by the establishment of definite programs of accident prevention received serious attention by most managements.

The first move toward an organized safety movement in industry came at a convention of the Association of the Iron and Steel Electrical Engineers at Milwaukee in 1912. A session devoted to safety formed a committee that was charged with the duty of arranging for a larger meeting devoted wholly to safety, and to which all persons and groups with an interest in safety were to be invited. This meeting was held in New York city in October 1913. It formed an organization named the National Council for Industrial Safety whose scope was limited to the promotion of safety in industry, but at its 1915 convention the name was changed to National Safety Council and its scope broadened to include accident prevention for the entire population, on the streets and highways, in the schools, homes, everywhere.

National safety council

Interest in safety is the primary requirement for Council membership as well as for attendance at its Congresses. Most of its members are manufacturing companies, public utility companies, compensation and liability insurance companies, local safety councils, chambers of commerce, automobile clubs, and, by courtesy, schools and governmental agencies.

The Council seeks to promote safety largely through the compilation and dissemination of information on the causes of accidents and methods of preventing them. Much of the information is received directly from reports made by Council members, while other information is obtained by special surveys and studies made in industrial plants, on the highways, in specific branches of industry, etc. The information thus gathered is graphic posters, or by the development of detailed plants and programs for accident prevention. The Council does not manufacture, test, sell, or approve safety devices; neither does it inspect factories or write insurance. It maintains a staff of safety men of professional caliber who give information to the members. Its library on safety is the largest and most comprehensive in the nation.

The Council publishes a number of monthly magazines, each devoted to a branch of safety. The oldest and best known of these, National Safety News, started publication in 1919. Only the privately published Safety Engineering antedated the News. Safety Engineering began publication a couple of years earlier, but after the Second World War it was merged with a magazine on production and the name became Safety Maintenance and Production.

The high point of the Council's activities each year is its National Safety Congress. These congresses have grown steadily in the scope and coverage of their programs, in attendance, and in standing, nationally and internationally. They have been at the heart of the safety movement in America ever since their inception. Although there is great value in providing such a meeting-place and discussion center for all persons and groups interested in safety, their major contribution, particularly in the early formative years, has been to provide a source of inspiration for all who participated.

Although as already stated, top-level management interest was inspired chiefly by a desire to minimize cost, the real safety doers, the men on the firing line of the safety movement, were motivated primarily by their humanitarian instincts. Few top executives, directing their businesses from their big-city offices, ever saw the accident-caused human wreckage and suffering at firsthand. But their subordinates in the plants had to live with these things. No normal person could fail to be profoundly affected by what these men in high injury rate plants saw and experienced. They quickly became the core of the safety movement in private industry. Most of the rapid progress made during the first two decades of the safety movement, in working out and learning how to apply the practical methods and techniques of accident prevention, was the fruit of their dedicated fervor and untiring effort.

The Council leadership quickly realized that the value and effectiveness of its work would depend chiefly on the extend to which interest and participation was developed at the local levels throughout the country, that is, in individual plants and in the respective communities. Accordingly, it continually urged and actively promoted the formation of community councils and the development of continuing safety programs in each and every plant and establishment throughout industry.

Community councils

The first community councils depended wholly on the voluntary services of already busy men, but it was soon found that for effective functioning, at least some full-time personnel were necessary. The Pittsburgh, Pennsylvania, council employed the first full-time salaried manager in 1917.

The council movement grew steadily, so that by 1950 there wee some 500 community, area, or state councils of which about half had full-time salaried personnel. In some cases, for example, in the Greater New York Safety Council, the staffs were of substantial size.

The activities of these councils cover in toto a very broad field, of course tailored more or less to the needs and conditions in their respective communities or areas. Their basic purpose is the promotion of safety interest and safety activities together with the spreading of good safety practices. A complete detailed listing would require too much space for inclusion herein, but their chief activity is the promotion of, planning for, and the servicing of safety meetings for any and all groups and interests, ranging from small evening or luncheon meetings to annual congresses patterned after the annual National Congress. In short, each such council functions, as far as its facilities permit, as the center of safety activities in its area.

Other agencies rendering safety services

There are literally hundreds of these agencies. A large number of trade and industry associations render a safety service primarily to their membership, but in some cases they go well beyond that, usually in the form of cooperative effort with safety councils or other groups. A few, notably The Portland Cement Association, have participated in the organized safety movement since its inception and have also been very active in promoting and servicing continuing safety programs in individual establishments in the various branches of industry. The notable reductions in combined membership injury rates that some of the industries so served have scored have been largely due to these Association programs.

United states bureau of mines

This bureau was established in 1910 in the Department of the Interior. One of its major functions is to study the causes of accidents and ill health among miners and to promote the application of preventive measures. Its work has been and continues to be outstanding in its field. A very large part of the reduction in the injury rate in the mining industry is certainly to be credited to the work of the Bureau. Its most spectacular accomplishment has been in coal mining. That industry, formerly marked by frequent explosions involving heavy loss of life and very high injury rates from other accidents as well, has become a relatively safe industry when its intrinsically hazardous nature is taken into account. The Bureau soon discovered the causes of coal mine explosions and proved them preventable. It developed rescue methods and provided trained crews with the specialized equipment necessary. Its first aid courses have helped to promote interest in safety, not only in the coal mining industry, but throughout industry in general. The Bureau also maintains a coal mine but since its inspectors are highly competent and armed with authority to enter and inspect, their findings and recommendations are taken very seriously indeed.

Bureau of labour statistics

Established in 1913, this bureau among other things collects, tabulates, and disseminates statistical information about occupation-injuries. It issues annual reports on them, giving estimated annual totals and breakdowns by branch of industry. It supplements these with reports on specific branches of industry.

National bureau of standards

An important function of this bureau, established in the Department of the Interior in 1910, is to develop safety standards for various materials and equipment and to formulate testing methods for determining their safety. The total volume of its accomplishments in the fields of fire and accident prevention bulks large. It works very closely with the American Standards Association, sponsoring many of the standards itself.

Bureau of labor standards

The objectives of this bureau, established as a division in 1934 and later raised to bureau status, are to formulate labor standards in labor legislation and labor law administration, and also to promote the improvement of working conditions. Its safety activities as a part of this general purpose include cooperating in the development and promotion of American Safety Standards through ASA procedure, furnishing consulting service on safety to labor administrative agencies and labor organizations, aiding states, upon request, to improve the competency of their safety personnel, and, in general, cooperating in the movement to reduce the toll of occupational injuries. The Bureau played a major part in the promotion of safety in federal employment. In 1940 the Bureau organized the Committee for the Conservation of Manpower in the War Industries, whose basic purpose was to make available to plants lacking adequately trained safety personnel, and unable to afford it, a competent safety advisory service through the part-time use of safety engineers loaned for the purpose by large plants able to spare them for perhaps a day per week as a contribution to the war effort.

Safety training courses

In-plant safety training has long been recognized as a basic element in any well-rounded safety program, but our educational authorities have been slow to add safety courses to their curricula, partly because they are loath to add to already overcrowded schedules and partly because of lack of demand from industry, which in general prefers to merge its safety training and indoctrination with the job training. Despite many years of promotional effort by a committee of the American Society of Safety Engineers, only a handful of schools of any nature were offering safety courses by 1940. In that year the accelerating demand for technically trained personnel led to initiation of the nationwide program of engineering-science-management training known as the ESMDT courses. These were federally financed, administered by the United States Office of Education, and given by the colleges and technical schools. The first course on industrial safety under this program was a 150-classroom-hour course given by the University of Pennsylvania, with the cooperation of the Philadelphia Safety Council, the Philadelphia Chapter of the American Society of Safety Engineers and the Bureau of Labor Standards of the U.S. Dept. of Labor. It was so successful, and there was so much demand for such courses, that a 96-classroom-hour course based on it was made available on a national basis. Over 150 colleges and technical schools cooperated in this program, and by its termination at war's end over 70,000 industrial personnel had completed its 96-hour course and many of them an advanced course of similar length as well.

Although these courses were for key men, foremen, job bosses, safety committeemen, etc., in industry and required only a grade school education, the experience influenced many of the colleges to serious consider adding safety courses to their curricula. The National Safety Council made grants to four colleges to help them to make a start. These and a few others added experienced safety engineers to their faculties to organize the courses and teach them, thus meeting the problem of lack of safety knowledge by their regular teaching staff. This arrangement was acceptable since these were not credit courses. After the war a few colleges developed qualified instructors, and with the help of a committee of A.S.S.E., obtained the accreditation of safety courses to be offered as electives, particularly in their engineering curricula. The number of colleges offering accredited safety courses has grown slowly. Future growth will be governed by demand from industry, primarily.

There are two reasons for this. Despite the general use of the term engineer in this connection, there is little engineering in the safety field. Very few problems the safety man meets in the practice of his profession require a knowledge of basic engineering theory or formulae. Perhaps the more important reason is the fact that the overriding need is for a higher level of safety mindedness throughout our entire population. What better way can there be? In plants we use a wide variety of safety promotional and educational activities and should use them more, but young minds are far more easily influenced than are older ones. The great success a leading church has in holding its membership is credited by its spokesmen as very largely due to the teaching of its basic tenets in its schools. Why not follow a similar course for safety? It is a worthy cause also.

Some of the vocational schools have made encouraging progress along this line. Their work points the way to complete safety integration in our entire school system. It would be a big job but not an unduly difficult one. A prerequisite is to get adequate and suitable safety material into the texts and other teaching materials. Only a very few college texts, even those on production and engineering, contain any safety material whatever, and those that do usually present it as a separate chapter, so brief and superficial as to be of little value. This is not the fault of the authors. No author of a text will include material for which he receives little or no demand, nor will he devote sufficient time and effort to it to enable him to present its essentials in a sound ad well balanced fashion-one of the most difficult jobs such an author can undertake. However there is a way that is intensely practical. If only a few schools, preferably engineering colleges, would join forces with ASSE to make detailed studies of their texts, teaching materials and courses, decide where, and what, safety material should be included, few, if any, authors would fail to cooperate. Also, the ASSE would gladly recruit the services of safety engineers in the areas of the participating colleges to act as consultants to the faculty members on an "on call" basis. The integration structure should be capped by a tie-together and summation course offered as at least an elective in the senior year. For students wishing to make safety their profession, safety should either be a required major, or made the subject of a postgraduate year leading to a master's degree.

State safety services

Every state has created some agency charged with at least some responsibility for the safety of at least some of the employed persons in the state. Some have very broad and far reaching responsibility for the safety of at least some of the employed persons in the state. Some have very broad and far reaching responsibility, but as is the case with Workmen's Compensation, none include all. The names of these agencies vary among the different states, being referred to as Department of Labor, Department of Labor and Industry, Industrial Commission, etc. The first agency of this tỳpe in this country was the Department of Factory Inspection created in Massachusetts in 1867.

As previously pointed out, such agencies were created to enforce laws aimed at the correction of bad conditions or abuses connected with employment. The campaign that ultimately brought the widespread passage of workmen's compensation laws also usually brought companion legislation requiring the safeguarding of hazardous machinery and equipment. The basic approach was to secure correction through laws enforced by inspectors armed with police power. Penalty for non-compliance with corrective orders issued by the inspection agency is generally a fine, but in many states it can, in flagrant cases, include imprisonment also. Also in many states, the offending employer may be forbidden to operate the machine or equipment in question, or if the hazard is general, forbidden to operate the entire plant until the condition has been corrected.

In their early years, the state factory inspection services made a major contribution to the safety movement by getting machinery guarded and many other serious hazards corrected in plants whose managements would not do it of their own volition. The flow of injuries from such hazards decreased as the work of safeguarding progressed. By about 1930, the country-wide level of safeguarding was reasonably good, in the establishments subject to safety inspection, primarily in the manufacturing industries. although machinery continued to be and still is, a relatively important injury source, machinery injuries are now mostly due to faulty operation and maintenance and failure to comply with well-known rules of safe practice.

It may seem surprising to the objective minded onlooker, but instead of expanding their services to include phases of injury prevention other than mere guarding, most of the inspection agencies pushed for ever more extensive and detailed regulatory requirements. They lost sight of the fact that the sole purpose of the safety regulations and the inspection services that enforced them was to cut down the flow of injuries. They failed to keep sufficiently in touch with safety progress in even the plants they inspected, to realize that at least part of their efforts could be more productive if properly applied to activities other than the mere enforcement of safety regulations. Nor did they learn to think in terms of injury rates and how to find and reduce those rates that we higher than good practice permits. Instead, most of them gauged the value and quality of their inspection service chiefly by the number of inspections made and corrective orders issued and complied with year by year. Many of them still follow this course and justify their budgetary requests by such data, absurd as that appears to the prevention minded analyst.

A few inspection agencies have experimented with the so-called educational approach, holding safety meetings, sending out safety literature, etc., much as the community councils do, usually carrying on their enforcement work as a parallel activity but in at least one state practically giving it up. They failed to see the limitations of this approach, i.e., that only those already interested in safety will attend safety meetings, seek safety information, or read and make use of safety literature sent them unsolicited. Apparently they also failed to analyze the injury data in their respective states sufficiently to discover that by far the greater part of each year's injury total is contributed by small and very small employers, few of whom are sufficiently safety minded to want to find out the quality of their safety performance. These agency heads failed to realize that their problem was, and still is, to find ways and means of carrying the know how and practice of safety to those employers who do not have it and do not know that they lack it. Whatever gains the agencies using this approach may have scored have not been great enough to be discernible in the year by year injury totals of their respective states.

At least one state however, made a clear-headed analysis of its situation and has been experimenting with what it calls the "consultative approach." This involves broadening the plant inspection to a thorough-going appraisal of all phases of safety, such as guarding, safety of plant and equipment, of processes, of operating procedures, attention given to the development and observance of safe practice, safety promotional activities and so forth. Using the findings as a basis, the inspector functions as a consultant to the management, helping it to correct the weaknesses found and to develop and prosecute a well-rounded and sound safety program suited to its needs.

Enforcement authority is not surrendered; it is merely held in abeyance for use if a management fails to cooperate. In such case its direct value is, of course, limited to the correction of the hazards covered by the state safety regulations. Even with such uncooperative employers, however, this approach has considerable value because the recommendations of a competent man clothed with authority to enforce the applicable regulations will usually be treated with greater respect than they would if he had no such authority, or if they knew he wouldn't use it.

The right to enter and inspect at any reasonable hour is essential to the success of the consultative approach. If he cannot inquire into every phase of plant operation that might have a bearing on safety, the inspector-consultant will be seriously handicapped in advising soundly as to the kind and extent of corrective action that should be taken.

Enough success has been scored with this approach to show that if properly applied it can be very effective with high injury rate plants. In most states however, many difficulties will have to be overcome before it can be used extensively or with anything approaching full effectiveness. First of all, it takes very good men. The inspector-consultant must have a thorough knowledge of the hazards connected with the branches of industry in his area of responsibility and the means of their control. He must also have a similarly thorough knowledge of the methods and techniques of accident prevention in general. He must be able to present his findings clearly and convincingly. Finally, he must be a sound and effective salesman.

There are few such men in the state inspection services. this is not said in a spirit of criticism. Men of the competence required to make effective use of the consultative approach would be wasted as mere inspectors, nor could they be hired or long held for the salaries inspectors receive. In addition to the low salaries, there is in many states a still more serious obstacle, political appointment. Where political preference is requisite to get and hold such a job an effective service of this type is simply not possible. Should a fully competent man be appointed, which is highly unlikely, his first allegiance would be to his party or sponsor; his work would be a poor second.

Also, the safety laws of many states are faulty in one or more important respects. Most of them require at least an annual inspection of every establishment covered by them regardless of the quality of their safety performance. None recognize injury rate. From the standpoint of the injury preventionist it is obviously absurd for a state safety inspector to make his routine inspection of a great plant that through long years of systematic safety effort has brought its injury rate down to figures approaching zero, yet it is still the usual practice because "it is the law." Such laws were necessary and proper when they were enacted, mostly around the turn of the century, but they do not fit present conditions and should b amended to authorize the state inspection service to place its effort wherever it can get maximum results. Some state laws do not give adequate right of entry for the consultative approach or are too limited in their coverage. In effect, they say that an occupational injury in an establishment not covered by the law is of no concern to the state.

The lack of injury data adequate to furnish a measured of performance in any effort to cut down the year by year injury totals is another obstacle. In most states, injury reporting is required only for the administration of the workmen's compensation laws. The agencies administering them have the primary duty of seeing to it that the injured worker's interests are fully protected. hey have no official concern whatever with prevention and usually their quite natural practice is to hold to themselves all injury reports and al injury data until they are of no further use. By that time such data are of little value as a guide for preventive efforts. In some states, the law requires that such data be kept secret except for presentation in summary form in annual or biennial reports of the agency. Although the data on compensated injuries would not include employment data and therefore would not alone furnish a year by year or month by month measure of the over-all safety performance for the state, they could be made to do so if correlated properly with the employment data for the corresponding periods, usually compiled by another state agency or by the federal government or both.

Safety movement a complex of activities

The foregoing description of the development of the safety movement in industry gives only the highlights and even these in brief form only. Any reasonably complete description would require far too much space for inclusion herein. And for the same reason, the description of its current makeup has been held to the minimum deemed essential to the purposes of this text. Actually, it consists of an extensive complex of activities carried on by an even greater complex of groups and agencies of government (state, federal, municipal) safety councils, trade and industry organizations, professional engineering and technical societies, in-plant safety programs, and labor unions and groups. Each such agency or group or association is busily carrying on its own activities, often traditional rather than realistically suited to existing conditions, in its own little corner with no apparent interest in, or concern for, the magnitude or trend of the year by year injury totals.

This hodgepodge is the predictable result of the failure of management, labor, and the state agencies charged with the administration of safety and workmen's compensation laws to join hands in the formative years of the safety movement and work together toward a common goal. Had they done so and provided for joint, objective minded leadership with provisions for an annual appraisal of progress made and needs yet to be met, surely action would have been taken long since to extend good safety performance to the areas lacking it; and the annual injury and death totals would be far smaller than they are, probably halved, at least if we may judge from the progress made in areas where joint cooperative effort has been vigorously applied.

Neither the state safety agencies nor organized labor had any part in developing the methods and techniques of accident prevention or even any direct means of keeping in touch with the progress that was being made by, and within, the organized safety program in private industry. Of course, the National Safety Congresses and similar meetings have always been open to anyone who cared to attend and pay the moderate fees, if any. But such attendance would ordinarily be as individuals at their own expense. Few, either from the state agencies or organized labor, were in a position to attend had they wanted to in view of the fact that neither they nor their agencies could have any voice in policy matters. This was most unfortunate, for joint participation of these three major groups, management, labor, and state and federal government, would have been highly constructive particularly during those early formative years. Their failure to get together was due chiefly to the mutual bitterness and hostility engendered by the long struggle that finally brought state safety and workmen's compensation laws. Labor was bitter because of the long and sometimes ruthless resistance to its demands for what it regarded as the minimum of simple justice for the injured workers and their dependents.

It is only fair to point out here that there was relatively little employer opposition to workmen's compensation for several reasons. Perhaps the most important was that it was quickly realized that the cost would bear on each employer in accordance with his accident experience and, as such experience accumulated, would become a calculable cost item. Also it would become insurable on an actuarially sound basis. Furthermore, many employers were sick of the ambulance chasing setup, the uncertainty of it all as well as the unfavorable publicity that was so frequently involved. They were willing to accept almost anything that would bring relief from these annoyances. Finally, and by no means least, many employers sympathized with the accident victims and were in favor of suitable corrective action.

Employers naturally fought safety laws that included requirements they thought unnecessary or unduly expensive, thoroughgoing power transmission machinery guarding in particular. In those days a large plant using a large number of power driven machines might have literally thousands of feet of shafting and many hundreds of drive belts. In such a plant guarding all the power transmission machinery would be a major expense of itself; usually, too, there were other hazards that required expensive safe-guarding, for few had given any worthwhile attention to hazard elimination. Since an unsafe act, or at least not adequately safe action, by the accident victim was almost always an obvious factor, employers were slow to accept the now well-established principle that it is the employer's duty to do everything he reasonably can to keep his employees free of injury while at their work for him regardless of faulty behavior on their part.

Some employers fought inspection laws for another important reason that was perhaps justified at the time. It was before the advent of merit service in state agencies and they feared inspection by political appointees who would be unlikely to have any practical knowledge of industrial plants and equipment and who, therefore, might issue orders that were impractical, unnecessary, or unduly expensive. In those days, too, many plant managements were openly in politics; inspectors of the opposite party could make things difficult indeed. Thus, many employers fought the passage of the laws in the first place, and later fought many of the orders issued under them. All this created an attitude of mutual dislike and hostility between the inspection services and many, perhaps most, of the employers. In some areas at least, it persists in some degree to this day.

In some states the quality of the inspection service fully justified management fears but in others the service was reasonably efficient and objective from the start and such weaknesses as appeared were soon corrected, although such corrections were usually in the direction of ever stricter enforcement. Other faults, such as ambiguity, impractical requirements, and conflicting provisions, caused much trouble also. Often, orders issued by different inspectors on the same hazard were at variance or even in direct conflict. This applied also as between different states, a matter of very real importance to a company having plants in more than one state. Some good came out of this situation, however. It highlighted the value of uniform guarding requirements and led to the setting up of a means for their development under American Standards Association procedure.

Statewide safety programs

The failure of the President's Conference to develop a nationwide program need not mean that there is no hope of accelerating the present slow rate of progress in cutting injury rates and totals. Undoubtedly any sound national safety program would be based on action at the state level, that is, statewide programs operated by the respective states with the national organization functioning in an advisory and service capacity. But many individual states can, if they will, set up statewide programs that would get results if properly organized and vigorously prosecuted.

It has been clearly shown, by results attained, that if the consultative approach is properly applied by competent men who have authority to enter, inspect, and enforce where necessary, it is very effective in improving safety performance in high injury rate establishments and businesses. Since only the state factory inspection agencies have such authority and also have, or could well be given, the necessary manpower, the setting-up of statewide programs based on these consideration is the best and most promising plan of action.

The consultative approach is time consuming; the great number of employers that must be effectively reached in even the lesser states means that, in most states at least, an impossibly large field force would be needed to service them all in anything short of several yeas. But experience has shown that properly led and serviced safety activities by volunteers on a part time or off-hour basis or both, can make many conversions also. Therefore, each state program should be made up of a well-knit complex of these two kinds of activities combined in a manner suited to the needs and conditions of the state in question.

Presumably the organizational setup of a state program may vary considerably as to detail, but three things are viewed as essential to successful performance, i.e., (a) that the full-time personnel, including the executive head, be under merit service, (b) that the organizational leadership be sound and objective minded, (c) that it have sufficient standing to get the needed non-partisan political and public support to, first, establish the program and then to carry it "on faith" until it has proved itself.

There have been several attempts to set up such statewide safety programs but none have endured, partly because the necessary preliminary steps were not taken and partly because of the failure of the key groups, labor, employers, the state inspection services and the safety leadership in the state to compose their traditional differences and, in some cases, dislikes sufficiently to cooperate wholeheartedly in developing and prosecuting such a project. Nevertheless, enough progress has been made to make it clear that such programs, properly set up and pushed, would get very worthwhile results.

An objectively made safety appraisal is an absolute necessity if the action program is to be much more than guesswork. The high injury rate establishments and branches of industry must be discovered and the means of reaching them most effectively determined. Existing safety services must be evaluated and those of maximum effectiveness for this work expanded if possible. Agencies and groups able to expand their current safety activities that are productive or take on additional ones should be urged to do so and aided thereto.

Predictions as to the future

Prediction is a hazardous pastime. This is particularly

true for industry in times of rapid change and expanding technology. A steady, high rate of orderly industrial activity favors safety. Fluctuations in volume of production, changes in methods and processes, shifting employment, unrest-these things and the like, bring higher injury rates. On the other hand, there is considerable evidence that public awareness and concern over the seriousness of our accident wastage is growing. Safety in its varied forms is slowly but surely being integrated into our educational system; it is increasingly included in radio and television programs; professional safety engineers are increasing in number and in degree of professional organization; the American Society of Safety Engineers grows steadily in size and standing.

Perhaps the greatest hope of reducing the annual injury and death totals lies in the growing interest and participation in safety activities by organized labor. Labor unions are progressively increasing their safety activities, particularly by establishing safety departments having the dual purpose of promoting safety interest and safety know how among the membership and transforming the currently most passive support into active interest and participation on as wide a scale as possible. Organized labor with its millions of workers at the firing-line source of work injuries and its tremendous political strength could unquestionably do much to improve the situation in at least every state and community where it is strong and soundly led. However, unless such action and the policies under which it is prosecuted, are based on an objective, clear-headed appraisal of the conditions and needs in each state in question, and, further, unless any and all traditional animosities and prejudices between the participating groups can be buried and forgotten for the good of the cause, accomplishment will be limited at best. In other words, it is a job that can be done but will it be? What do you think?

10

Staffing and Controlling

Human Resources Planning

Historically, people have been hired and trained on an "as needed" basis. This approach can be a handicap in today's rapidly changing world. Consequently, many organizations have developed comprehensive human resource plans that focus on business objectives as a foundation for planning personnel needs. Executives must anticipate personnel needs so that the right numbers and kinds of people are hired to avoid hindering business opportunities. At the same time, a balance must be maintained to avoid overstaffing, which can be wastefully expensive. Applicants should be hired who show high potential for growth. Management is wise to cultivate loyalty and facilitate a career path by providing education, training, and work experience opportunities. This is an investment. Human resource planning not only analyzes present talent in light of future needs, it also anticipates vacancies due to promotions, dismissals, resignations, retirements, and so forth. Careful planning is required so that the most qualified people can be placed in critical positions and emergency replacements can be made quickly. This planning is an immense aid during normal growth, acquisitions, and other changes.

Computerized personnel inventories are used by a growing number of organizations. A data bank is compiled that contains each employee's name and background, including data on experience, training, education, and seniority. Within a few seconds, for example, a human resources executive can obtain a printout of employees soon to retire and those most likely to be promoted.

Human Resources Accounting

The essence of human resource accounting is the concept that employees have a quantifiable value to an organization that should be studied prior to management and personnel decisions. Proponents claim that it can be shown specifically how important human resources are to an organization more attention would be given to personnel administration decisions. A number of 'techniques for'quantifying human resources are available. With the historical cost method, the recruiting, training, and other costs for each employee are recorded, capitalized, and amortized over the employee's expected tenure. When the employee leaves, the unamortized balance of the investment is written off as a loss. The replacement cost approach is self-explanatory. The present value method analyzes the contributions of the employee by studying salary and productivity. These methods are relatively new, and they are being refined.'

What are the implications of human resource accounting for security programs? As part of a prosecution and termination decision, the security executive, if he or she is truly business-oriented, should consider these quantitative approaches to expose actual costs. These techniques are also helpful for illustrating a return on investment for protection personnel. Senior executives are likely to be impressed with such a business approach.

Careful human resource planning is required in the face of changing demographic and social trends. The post—World War II boom is one such trend; workers in this age group are striving for the limited number of management positions available. This problem is compounded because older workers are staying in the workforce longer and because increasing numbers of minorities, including women, are gaining a stronger foothold in management positions.

Contemporary workers' values are changing, which is reflected in demands for enriched jobs and flexible work schedules. Thus, security managers should enrich security jobs whenever possible through such techniques as job rotation and job enlargement, job rotation attempts to reduce boredom, a significant problem in security work. For those of us who have filled a stationary post for endless hours or have endured whole shifts in front of CCTV monitors until we could not see what we were looking at this problem is easy to comprehend. The wise protection executive rotates personnel among patrols, posts, control center duty, and so forth, job enlargement also helps to reduce boredom while lowering turnover* and increasing job satisfaction and a feeling of accomplishment. It basically involves giving a worker more do. For example, instead of assigning security officers to routine patrols with watchclocks, enlarge their job by having them complete a checklist on security, safety, and fire protection.

The compressed work Week is gaining momentum. Examples are ten-hour days for four days or, for those on a thirty-six-hour work week, twelve hours daily for three days. With flextime—another scheduling variation gaining in popularity-employees choose their own work hours. Core hours may be required so that everyone is at work during certain times. Obviously, such schedules are not appropriate for all organization, and longer work days may increase on-the-job fatigue. However, the benefits are reduced commuting time, more personal time for leisure, and greater job satisfaction. Personnel are likely to appreciate their jobs more and improve their performance when their lifestyle is enhanced.

Specifications for the Job

Effective personnel selection is crucial to organizational effectiveness. To select the best possible person for a job, management should compare applicants with specifications established for the job. This approach deserves more attention than it usually receives, because knowing what to look for helps managers decide how and where to recruit and who would make the best employee. Furthermore, specifications increase objective decision making while curbing biases.

Job specifications typically pertain to experience, education, training, and personality. Care must be exercised with whatever guidelines are used in the selection process; otherwise, litigation can result. Two important guidelines are to ensure that selection criteria are job-related nondiscriminatory.

Experience

Near the very top of the list of criteria for hiring is experience. When an individual has done the job before and is familiar with the reality of the working environment, a certain skill has been obtained. The experience gained through mistakes and successes often gives an applicant insight into the most appropriate ways to reach objectives. With the variety of existing security and loss prevention positions, management must carefully decide on the type and years of experience required.

The debate continues over the recruitment of public safety or military personnel for S&LP positions. These veterans usually have good training and experience, which can add expertise to a protection program. The ultimate question besides the widely held biases about such individuals is whether the applicant can fit into the organization and its objectives. Questions of concern are how the applicant views security in the private sector and what strategies the applicant would recommend to deal with private sector crime. These questions and quality applicant screening methods will increase the chances that an individual will "fit" the organization.

Education

A college education is not the absolute answer to success at any job. Higher education is only one of a handful of qualifications that produce a well-rounded employee. Experience, training, and a good personality ability to get along with others) are also factors in producing a well-qualified job applicant. If any one of these four factors is missing, an individual is likely to be hampered in his or her career.

Whereas training has a tendency to deal with "how," education deals with "why." The theories studied at educational institutions provide a foundation for what is put into practice.. Theory and practice complement each other, and answers come from the study of both. '

Most managers in security and loss prevention positions should possess a four-year college degree in a relevant field of study. Throughout this book, emphasis has been placed on interdisciplinary study, since many fields provide answers to protection problems. Examples are business management, risk management, accounting, and data processing.

Depending on the organization and the position, education may be de-emphasized as a criterion, for a security position. For instance, management may believe that the job can be accomplished better without a more expensive college educated individual. The management perspective may be* that an educated person is not needed for the job and that such a background would increase turnover. It is interesting that a large, nationally known contract security firm has a job application form (for security officer positions) that does not have any questions pertaining to training or education. Such entry level security positions obviously have different requirements from those for management positions.

Training and Education

A professional seeks out training and continuing education opportunities. This is where new ideas are gathered, present skills are sharpened, and newer skills are developed. The American Society for Industrial Security is an example of an organization at the forefront of continuing education in the S&LP field; protection experts conduct specialized programs throughout the United States. Colleges and universities also offer excellent programs. Security periodicals contain advertisements from a variety of firms involved in meeting training needs.

Job applicants in the protection field should be queried about completed courses, training, seminars, conferences, workshops, and the like. The applicant who asks about upgrading opportunities as part of the compensation package is a genuine professional.

Personality

Temperament, patience, assertiveness, and perseverance are some of the factors that characterize an individual's personality. It is difficult to appraise a candidate's total personality accurately during the screening process. References can supply some information, and psychological testing is often used for sensitive security positions. People with violent tendencies or psychological problems must be purged from the pool of applicants. Because security and loss prevention positions are basically people-oriented, practitioners must have excellent human relations skills. Some experts argue that personality tests are being used km because difficulty of linkiling scores to desired jab-behaviour. Questions pertaining to validity, reliability, job-relatedness, and discrimination are an important part of personnel testing. Later discussion will go into greater depth on issues.

The Certified Protection Professional

Another increasingly useful criterion for selecting an S&LP executive is the professional designation Certified Protection Professional (CPP), administered by the American Society for Industrial Security (ASIS). Requirements include endorsement by a CPP, a specific combination of experience and education, passing a one day examination, and affirmation of adherence to the CPP Code of Professional Responsibility. The CPP designation is another professional accomplishment that helps illustrate the competence of the practitioner.

Job Descriptions

Job descriptions are an immense aid to the executive when planning staffing decisions have to be made; however, many programs lac important attribute. The benefits of job descriptions are as follows:

- Budget requests are made easier when positions can be justified through complete descriptions of the jobs being performed.
- Job duties can be analyzed to make sure a protection program fits an organization's needs.
- Job specifications, recruitment, applicant screening, rates of pay, and other factors can be better prepared when reference is made to job descriptions.
- Job descriptions help subordinates and superiors understand each other better.

— Training is enhanced when it is relevant to the job to be performed.

A job analysis provides a foundation for a job description. Information is obtained by sending questionnaires to superiors and subordinates, by interviewing them, and by observing the job as it is being performed. The job description summarizes what the job entails. Categories relevant to the job description are job title, subordinate to, functions, and duties and responsibilities.

Analyzing jobs and preparing job descriptions are not easy tasks. Practitioners who are unfamiliar with the process may want to seek assistance from human resource specialists. The effort expended on such a project is sure to make the manager's job easier when other relevant tasks arise.

Recruitment

The basic purpose of recruitment it is to attract applicants who have the background and qualifications to assume vacant positions. There are several sources for job applicants. A company's own personnel is one major source. Hiring from within has several advantages: it is less expensive, motivation and morale are strengthened, and good performance is easier to verify. An outsider may look good on paper but may not be able to handle the job or may have an undesirable personality. Conversely, internal applicants may not have the skills or fresh ideas needed for a specific job.

In-house publications and bulletin boards are useful for posting openings. Management may encourage employees to inform their friends and relatives about job opportunities. But some equal opportunity programs prohibit businesses from giving jobs to people because of friendship.

In the recruitment of qualified applicants, help wanted advertisements must be carefully worded and must be used as a tool to avoid complaints of discrimination. The key is to dissuade job seekers who are not qualified for the position. This is accomplished by including in the advertisement attractive and unattractive features of the job, years of experience required, type of education and specific skills required, and job duties.

College recruiting is worth while for entry level or management trainee positions. Two-year colleges, four-year colleges, and universities typically have an ample supply of security, criminal justice, or business majors who are eager for experience. The protection executive should maintain close contact with educators, not only to obtain top-notch graduates, but also for research assistance.

Summer internships enable management to "preview" students before offering full-time employment. The recruitment of minorities is facilitated through such programs.

By attending trade conferences, recruitment efforts can be expanded as the practitioner makes contact with old and new friends. This relates to the "old boy" network, whereby informal associations provide a source for both solutions to problems and potential employees.

Private employment agencies and executive recruiting firms are two additional avenues to obtaining qualified people. However, since several other strategies are available to locate applicants, and with the possibility of having to pay up to one year's salary to these businesses, such firms should be used as a last resort.

Selection Techniques

The importance of selection techniques cannot be

overstated. Considerable efforts and resources are often expended to hire, presumably, the best possible individual for the organization. Management must implement quality job applicant screening process to prevent a mistake in hiring.

From a cost standpoint, the most expensive screening technique should be conducted last; for example, an application form is less expensive than a physical examination. As applicants progress through the screening steps, and as more and more applicants are found to be ineligible, fewer individuals will require the more costly screening methods.

The Resume

Once a job opening has been advertised or communicated, resume begin to arrive and must be evaluated. The typical resume includes experience and education; it is a summary of an individual's professional accomplishments.

How prevalent is the falsification of resumes? Experts estimate that as many as 30 percent of resumes contain falsified information.' Many people believe that their qualifications are not good enough to complete, or they see themselves as better than they really are. Consequently, these job seekers take a chance on an employer's superficial and perfunctory applicant screening methods.

The Application Form

Since there are so many different styles of resumes, an application form provides uniformity of questions and answers. Some businesses may require answers to certain questions before deciding to interview an applicant.

Those who review applications should be familiar with signs of deception. The term "self-employed" is sometimes used by job seekers to hide periods of unemployment or institutionalization. Not signing an application is another red flag that may signal deception. Since Social Security numbers are issued by state, knowledge of the numbering by state can expose inconsistencies in an applicant's background.

Many job seekers do not realize that the application form is an important screening tool for employers. The ability to follow directions and organize thoughts, neatness, spelling, sentence structure, and truthfulness all reflect on the applicant's work habits. And these factors go beyond the actual content of the answers.

Properly used by employers, these forms are among the best predictors of job success, especially when questions are scored as if they were test questions.[7] Through data collected from applications, a company can study whether those with no background in security do better or worse than those with a few years' experience. Decisions based on application form data should be supported by good research. Simply to assume that those with no experience will do worse than those with experience can lead to a charge of discrimination. An organization should maintain records on employee performance to justify its decisions.

Personnel Tests and Legal Requirements

Management should plan carefully before using personnel tests. What is the cost of testing? Would employee selection without the test be satisfactory? Is the test discriminatory? How would the test improve the overall quality of the workforce?

A wide variety of tests are available to measure job applicants; the quality varies. Validity and reliability are two very important factors to consider when selecting tests. Validity means that the testing instrument is measuring what is intended. When a typist position needs to be filled, the test offered to applicants must measure typing skills. Reliability means that the instrument provides consistency of measurement that repeat tests produce similar results,

Because some personnel tests can discriminate against minorities, the Equal Employment Opportunity Commission (EEOC) and the Office of Federal Contract Compliance have acted upon unfair tests. Public, private, and non-profit organizations must take steps to validate tests so that it can be test scores correlate with job success. Validation methods are not as complicated as many employers believe. Basically, test scores are collected upon hiring but are kept separate from personnel decisions. Later, success on the job is objectively measured and correlated with tests used during hiring. Another method, concurrent validity coefficient, measures the relationship between test scores of present employees and their success at that time. A third approach is validity generalization. It is based on the view that if characteristics of a job are similar among several locales, the same test can be used in all locales, provided that the test has been validated in at least one situation. This is a widespread approach supported by court ruling.

One of the most often cited cases dealing with employer testing is Griggs v. Duke Power Co., 915 Sup. Ct. 849 (1971). In 1968, several employees of the Duke Power Company in North Carolina were given a paper and pencil test for manual labour. Willie Griggs and other black workers sued Duke Power, claiming job discrimination under the Civil Rights Act of 1964. They argued that the paper and pencil test was not job-related. The Supreme Court agreed and stated that a test is inherently discriminatory if it is not job-related and differentiates on the basis of race, sex, or religion.

Subsequent to the landmark Griggs case, an intimidating number of EEOC and Office of Federal Contract Compliance guidelines on employee selection procedures evolved into the 1978 Uniform Guidelines on Employee Selection Procedures, which were jointly adopted by the EEOC, the Civil Service Commission, and the U.S. Departments of Labour and justice.' The purpose of the Uniform Guidelines is to meet the need for a uniform set of principles concerning the use of tests and other selection methods. In essence, all selection procedures must be valid, job-related, and nondiscriminatory. This includes background investigations, employment inter~, views, tests, and so forth. The EEOG regards all screening methods as "tests", that have the potential to discriminate.

During fiscal 1985, the EEOC and state and local agencies received 119,695 charges of discrimination. The EEOC alone received 72,002 charges of employment discrimination, resolving 63,567 through administrative processes. Hundreds of court actions were also filed. A record $54 million in awards was recovered through litigation for victims of discrimination by the EEOC.

Many security executives favour the use of written honesty tests and psychological tests. The Reid Report, for example, is a written honesty test that reveal an individual's trustworthiness and attitude toward honesty. Validity and reliability studies supporting honesty tests have been published in scholarly journals. Honesty tests help avoid the legal problems that may be encountered with use of the polygraph.

The Minnesota Multiphasic Personality Inventory (MMPI) a popular psychological test-reveals habits, fears, sexual attitudes, depression, and symptoms of mental ill. A built-in ' lie ' scale exposes those who try to falsify answers. The MMPI has been revised in an attempt to eliminate any adverse impact on minorities.

Job candidates are becoming particularly knowledgeable about and tests relevant legal guidelines. The Buros Institute of Mental Measurement (University of Nebraska), an evaluator of published tests, reports that many job candidates contact the institute to request information about the validity of tests. The Buros Institute is analogous to a consumers' evaluation service for psychological tests of all types. Employers also contact this institute for assistance in choosing tests. The best tests are those developed by qualified test publishers that can provide strong evidence of test validity and reliability. The Buros Institute publishes the Mental Measurements Yearbook which evaluates published tests."

The Primary Interview

The interview is a major tool used by employers to select employees. Its strength as a universally applied screening technique contrasts sharply with the criticism of researchers who attack the validity and reliability of the interview. Critics argue that employment interviews have low reliability and validity because interviewers often ask "the same old questions"—for example, "What are your strengths?" "What are your weaknesses?" Since such standard questions surface repeatedly, job applicants are prepared for subsequent interviews with memorized answers. Consequently, the interviewer learns less about the applicant. Another problem with interviews is that the applicant may be "packaged real nice" but does an awful job when hired. The use of multiple screening tools eliminates such problems.

The realistic job preview is an approach used to curb the practice of an organization presenting itself in a positive light when the truth is to the contrary. Such inaccuracies foster job dissatisfaction, contempt, and turnover. The interview should be a time to discuss realistic job expectatations.

Interviewers and interviewing techniques vary greatly. One way to establish a degree of uniformity in interviewing is through the structured approach, in which questions are carefully prepared, written, and followed. A standardized form aids this process.

The following strategies are suggested for interviewers:

— Plan the questioning.

— Ask the same questions to all interviewees to compare answers.

— Try to ask unique questions to prevent the interviewee from responding with memorized answers to common questions.

— Ask open-ended questions requiring a lengthy response to learn more about the applicant.

— Listen attentively.

— Do not jump to conclusions.

— Avoid allowing one or two responses to affect the overall rating of the appilcant.

— Use silence if necessarv after certain Questions are answered to eticit more information.

— Be aware of nonverbal communication, which may be more revealing than verbal communication.

— Be tactful with interviewing techniques, since security and loss prevention professionals are often familiar with these methods.

The Background Investigation

Three major purposes of the background investigation are to verify the information provided by the applicant, to ascertain performance in previous jobs, and to obtain additional information of a positive or negative nature.

The average job seeker will be positive, and many have an inclination toward exaggeration. Since a job applicant is "selling" himself or herself, often for a better position at a higher salary, much is at stake in our competitive world; education, experience, skills, and accomplishments are often embellished. Moreover, background information of a negative nature is usually not volunteered. A poor hiring decision can result in reduced productivity, lowered morale, and damaged internal and external relations. The court system is increasingly imposing liability on employers for the actions of their employees. Courts are ruling that employers owe a duty to the public to exercise care and diligence in screening and supervising workers.

Since protection, personnel are in critical positions, whereby their actions can save or doom an enterprise, the background investigations of these applicants must be thorough. In fact, the applicant can obtain a view of the level of security maintained by the employer by being on the receiving end of the applicant screening process.

Those who conduct numerous background investigations are familiar with the "tricks of the trade." For instance, by obtaining references from sources provided by the applicant, a more in-depth investigation is possible. Letters of reference should be carefully analyzed. They are not always reliable. Educators may write a letter of reference for a student they know only superficially. Family friends may write such letters. Employers often provide positive letters because they fear being sued or want to get rid of an undesirable employee. Also, consider the possibility of an applicant forging background documents and placing them in the employer's mail system.

A thorough knowledge of applicable laws is necessary for those who conduct background investigations. Since 1966, Congress and state legislatures have passed many bills outlining citizen rights.

Applicants being investigated should be informed about the check what will be checked. A release form is appropriate, signed by the app and giving permission to the investigator to conduct inquiries into p records (e.g., credit reports, college transcripts, medical records). out the release form, public records are often sought in the back investigation.

If in-house specialists are unavailable, consider hiring a firm that specializes in background investigations. The applicant should be notified of such an investigation and the areas of inquiry, and the employer should obtain a release form prior to such an investigation so that private records can be checked.

Public Records

Public records enable employers to obtain sound, relevant facts about applicants at a low cost. Four types of records are particularly helpful: criminal records, workers' compensation claims histories, driving records, and college and university degree verifications.

' Criminal records are widely available. According to the National Employment Screening Services over 90 percent of the nation's counties and parishes will conduct a search for felony convictions for employers, and most will do it at no charge. About one-third will provide results over the telephone, and the rest will respond by mail, it is vital to obtain all previous addresses from the applicant, since one missing address may be the jurisdiction where a criminal conviction occurred.

Workers' compensation claims histories provide information on whether the job seeker can handle a physically or mentally demanding position. The NESS reports that forty-five states make these records available to employers for screening job applicants. Forty states provide the records at no charge.

Driving records provide considerable data: name, address, date of by physical description, physical limitations, possibly Social Security number, and violations of traffic laws. A substance abuse problem and/or a desired for safety may be revealed. All states permit access to driving records for, employment screening purposes. The cost is minimal.

Educational records, are public to the extent that an employer can call a~ college or university to inquire whether the job applicant attended and graduated. For further information, the Family Educational Rights and Privacy Act of 1974 prohibits anyone other than the applicant from receiving educational records. Therefore, if the employer is interested in these records, the job applicant should sign a release form so that they can be obtained. Since some applicants' educational claims are false, degree verification is important.

Another helpful source for staffing and personnel decisions is Employment Law in the 50 States: A Reference for Employers. This guide covers laws such of each state on such topics as drug testing, the polygraph, employee access to personnel records, employment at will, and whistle-blower protection.

Because background investigations can be expensive, especially for applicants who have lived in numerous locations, many employers use the polygraph to verify information and to save money. However, at the time of this writing, our political and social systems have generated considerable opposition to the polygraph as a job screening tool. Certain states prohibits its use to screen job applicants. The prudent executive is familiar with several types of screening methods without "putting all the eggs in one bask

The Physical Examination

Pre-employment physical examinations provide additional information for staffing decisions. These records are useful, not only for the selection process, but for other areas of personnel administration.

A thorough physical examination increases the chances that the chosen job applicant will become a productive employee. A poor decision in this regard could result in a considerable record of absences by the employee.

Personnel in the protection field should be physically fit. For example, fires and arrests are stressful events in which one's body is likely to be exerted. For those who lead a sedentary lifestyle or are overweight, a quick response to a physically demanding situation can lead to medical problems.

Another important reason for the physical examination is for subsequent comparison. At a later date, an employee may claim that job stress caused a medical problem. A comparison of records at the time of hiring with those contained in a disability claim will provide for a more equitable decision.

The physical examination does not guarantee that an employee will not have a heart attack in the next few years. But an exam helps to avoid liability if the employee's family sues, claiming that he or she should never have been hired for such a stressful position. The exam should show that the individual was in good health when hired.

Assessment Centers

Large organizations have their own assessment centers to improve decisions on internal and external job candidates. Smaller organizations can tap the resources of universities and consulting firms that serve several organizations at one time.

Basically, the purpose of an assessment, center is to study a group of applicants as they solve problems that they would encounter on the job. Then, the most successful individuals become leading job candidates. German military psychologists used the technique during World War II to improve their selection of leaders.

An assessment center uses well-prepared simulations based on specific jobs. Input from the workplace is at the foundation of simulation design. Well-trained observers and multiple assessment techniques are involved in standardized evaluations of behaviour. Situational tests are an excellent way for management to sample the behaviour of applicants in a situation resembling the actual work environment. These exercises must be carefully developed and tested. One test is the "in-basket": the applicant spends a few hours answering a superior's correspondence through problem solving and decision making on such topics as planning, organizing, delegating, and scheduling. Another exercise requires that the applicant study a problem, plan a solution, make a presentation, and ' then participate in a group discussion. Evaluators judge applicants on their knowledge, ingenuity, communications skill, and persuasiveness. The final decision on the best applicants must be a group decision by the evaluators. Several studies have demonstrated the validity of assessment center methodology. Experts in the behavioural sciences and management believe that this approach has a bright future.

These approaches to assessing abilities are appropriate for the selection of protection executives. Numerous problems face practitioners, so it would not be difficult to design "in-basket" predicaments or protection problems of a general nature. The case problems at the ends of the chapters in this book could be a source. Perhaps someday the Certified Protection Professional examination conducted by the American Society for Industrial Security will change from multiple-choice questions to case problems. Numerous examinations for professional designations are oriented toward problem solving in order to ascertain skills and abilities.

Quality Staffing

An employer's need to screen workers adequately versus the individual's right to privacy is a confrontation that is gaining momentum. Compounding the friction are new methods and technology to weed out undesirables. Controversial areas include:

- Controversial areas include:
- Genetic screening for health defects
- Drug testing
- AIDS screening
- Polygraph tests
- Psychological stress evaluations (PSE)
- Closed-circuit television and computer surveillance of the workplacei to check on productivity

The RIA emphasizes that technology often puts management in a difficult position. The advantages of a test should be balanced against worker dissatisfaction.

Directing

The process of directing involves guiding subordinates to become moti to reach desired performance. A key factor in this management effort employees to have the right skills to accomplish tasks correctly. E workers possess a high level of motivation, backed up by superb dire organizational goals and objectives will not be attained if the employee skills are lacking. Quality training provides a foundation directing.

Training

Once a job applicant becomes an employee, the organization has a made a sizable investment to acquire the most appropriate individual. The next major process is socialization (i.e., a learning process that, it is produces an employee who is beneficial to the organization).' Training and examples set by superiors are prime strategies for quality socialization manner in which an employer responds to employee needs also impact on this process. Exit interviews are an invaluable source for elavuating the socialization process; feedback on training, examples superiors, motivation and morale, and losses provides management information for improvements.

In the security and loss prevention field, the training of per entails unique problems. For those businesses where turnover is low nature of protection necessitates comprehensive training, such an investment is typically effective. However, when we security businesses in general, where them is high turnover, an investment in quality training, unfortunately, does not make good business sense to many executives. At the same time, potential civil liability for negligent failure to train can be devastating. The plaintiff's case in a suit over negligent security almost always includes inadequate training. When a jury hears that a security officer received a nightstick, Mace, and a revolver with limited training, or none at all, the defendant is placed in a difficult position. Protection executives must also consider training nonsecurity employees. Businesses have a duty not to negligently increase the risk of harm to customers. For example, hotel desk clerks who dispense keys must maintain key control and must know basic emergency procedures. Retailers should be prepared for robbery, and they require training with an emphasis on safety for employees and customers. Unfortunately, many organizations continue to gamble by not investing in training.

What is training?

> Training is the process of altering employee behaviour and attitudes in a way that increases the probability of goal attainment. When training is properly conducted, learning occurs. Learning is the acquisition of skills, knowledge, and abilities that result in a relatively permanent change in behaviour.

Training has commendable goals but problems plague this tool for changing and controlling, employee behaviour. A clear picture of these problems is part of the foundation for improved training.

— Training is complex. There are many variables that shape people's rbehaviour. Those who plan training should make greater use of scientific methods to improve training.

— Those who plan training often do not spend enough time studying research on how people gather and use information during learning. This is known as human information processing (HIP). One relevant topic is right-brain and left-brain thinking. People who are "right-brained" tend to be more subjective and inductive, while those who are "leftbrained" tend to be more objective and deductive. The latter concentrate on facts and are oriented toward being practical. Research is continuing, and a viewpoint is mounting to incorporate such HIP into training and placement.

— Many training programs evolve from an emergency. In a rush to implement training, its quality goes down.

— Fads make it difficult to distinguish between genuinely good training programs and those of poor quality, Knowledge of scientific methods can help in evaluating training.

— Training is sometimes used to solve problems that would be better by other means. Motivation and morale problems are unlike be solved through training.

— Training programs require refinement: they might be more complicated than necessary, conducted at the wrong time, or in need of updating.

— Training programs are not always legally derensible, The legisiation applicable to personnel screening also applies to training. Employers must show the fairness and validity of both training and procedures for selecting employees for training. Organizations often require certain training before promoting employees. Consequently, training programs have the potential for discrimination.

Motivation

One of the first research targets for psychologists was motivation. The literature on this topic reveals many theories and ways in which it is conceptualized.

In any organization, we hear comments such as "He is just that person is aworkaholic." Because human behaviour and motivation So complex, these comments are simplistic. Theories of motivation, imperfect, attempt to explain the "whys" behind people's actions, formulation and testing of motivational theories is complicated by the that "people are motivated by many factors, and the same person can be motivated by different factors in different situations.

Theories of Motivation

Two major viewpoints on motivation are trait theory and environment theory. Trait theory views people as being born with a certain motivation, which remains stable. Many managers favour this theory how do we assess the level of motivation of an individual? Few tests been developed to answer this question. Results show some evidence differences in motivation can be quantified; however, responses can faked. "Though some tests (like the MMPI) have a bulletin scale to d faking, most do not. It would be nice if we could develop 'fakes questions to accurately assess motivation. To date, we have not been successful."'

Environmental theory points to situational factors in determining an individual's motivation, claiming that under the right circumstances and in the right setting, workers can be motivated. Environmental influence are studied to ascertain what factors (e.g., workplace design, rewards) motivate people.

Theories of motivation are sometimes more complex than the be they try to explain. And although all theories of motivation have some research support, no one theory has been declared the best of the group. Executives typically do not have time to review, the literature on motivation, study each theory, and then select the best ones to apply. The theories presented below reflect a practical orientation to aid protection executives in motivating subordinates and curbing losses.

Maslow's Hierarchy of Needs

Not many college graduates have completed a bachelor's degree in the social sciences or business without having studied Abraham Maslow's hierarchy of human needs.

This theory is discussed universally in textbooks that deal with human behaviour. For the protection executive, Maslow's views are important not only to improve the management of people, but also as a strategy to prevent internal theft.

Maslow holds that an individual is motivated toward satisfaction of needs at a particular level, beginning at the lowest level of the needs hierarchy. When an individual satisfies these needs, they no longer serve as motivators, so the individual moves up to the next level. An upward move can be interrupted when a lower-level need manifests itself and the individual must drop back to satisfy the lower-level need.

Maslow's hierarchy of human needs is described as follows, with practical suggestions:

Basic physiological needs. Survival needs like food, water, and the elimination of wastes can be satisfied with employer assistance. A well-run company cafeteria and clean lavatories are examples of ways to satisfy these needs.

Safety and security needs. This need relates to order in one's life. A person needs to feel free from anxiety and fear. Adequate wages, medical insurance, and workplace safety help to satisfy these needs.

Societal needs. The need to be loved and have friends. This need and the esteem need can be fulfilled by supervisors. A supervisor should praise a subordinate when appropriate. Employees should receive recognition and/or awards after completing a good job. Employee socials are also helpful.

Esteem and status needs. The need to be competent, achieve, and gain approval and respect.

Self-actualization needs. This need is at the top of the

hierarchy of needs. It signifies that a person has reached his or her full potential, whether the person is a janitor, housewife, doctor, or whatever. An organization and its superiors can do a lot in assisting an employee to fulfill this need.

Much criticism has been leveled at Maslow's views, mainly because his theory has not been substantiated through research efforts. Specifically, precise definitions of variables and guidelines for empirical tests are lacking. Theorists argue that the hierarchy is not really a theory but is a viewpoint based on logical and clinical in-sights into human nature.

Despite the criticism, Maslow has made a thoughtful contribution to the study of human behaviour. Managers should seek to discover what motivates individual subordinates and what level of the hierarchy is most important to each subordinate.

In reference to curbing internal their, if a manufacturing plant has dirty rest rooms, an awful cafeteria, inadequate workplace safety, and disrepectful supervisors, the chances are that these conditions (which are contrary to the needs hierarchy) will breed internal theft.

Goal Setting

This theory of motivation was selected, for discussion because of its relevance to management by objectives (MBO), which was explained earlier. Goals are at the foundation of goal-setting theory because they are the basis for motivation and they direct behaviour. An individual must be aware of goals, accept them, know how to accomplish them, and receive feedback to ensure that performance is targeted correctly. Although this theory contrasts with Maslow's view that people are motivated by innate needs, research on MBO and on goal-setting in general is quite supportive.

Organizational Behaviour Modification

B.F. Skinner, the father of behaviour modification, is a very influential psychologist. His well-known book, Beyond Freedom and Dignity, states that people's behaviour can be controlled by, using rewards, while the controlled person still feels free.' Behaviourists base their motivational views on the idea that behaviour followed by positive consequences tends to be repeated, and behaviour followed by negative consequences tends not to be repeated. Through clear statements of what behaviour is expected by subordinates and what rewards are forthcoming, managers can condition employees' behaviour.

The preferred term by behaviourists is reinforcement, as they make reference to motives. Reinforcement (i.e., rewards) is at the foundation behaviour modification. A primary focus of behaviourists is on how affect the strength of the action.

Literature on reinforcement theory refers to organizational behaviour, modification, which deals with the manipulation of reward in order to alter behaviour. This school of thought avoids the term motivating employees while seeking to modify employee behaviour in ways that support the organization. The OB Mod concept can be applied to a variety of areas, including management by objectives, personnel development, compensation, and organizational change. Reinforcement can be expressed through praise, criticism, promotions, a smile, a frown, or indifference. It is unfortunate that managers, by their inaction, are informing their subordinates that no matter what they do, the consequences are consistentno reinforcement.

For managers interested in OB Mod, some guidelines are listed here:

- — Positive reinforcement is more effective than negative reinforcement.
- — Rewards should follow desired behaviour as soon as possible.
- — Subordinates must know what constitutes the behaviour desired by superiors.
- — Feedback is vital to employees so that correct behaviour can continue and mistakes can be corrected.
- — When providing feedback to subordinates, avoid put-downs. Such negative management behaviour depresses and discourages employees. Whenever possible, make each person feel important and part of the team. This strengthens productivity and morale.

Leadership

Identifying and developing leaders is a major concern of businesses. The military also has a great interest in this subject, as shown by its funding of research projects on leadership. Research results guide management in the selection of leaders and provide direction for allocating resources to train and develop them.

After studying the following definition of leadership, the reader will understand why it is an important concept: "Leadership is the process of influencing others to achieve specific objectives in specific situations without the use of unduly coercive methods or techniques."[1] Although there are many other definitions, a key point among the various definitions is the process of directing subordinates to certain objectives without coercion.

Styles of Leadership

Compelling leadership relies on authority, power, rules,

and threats. The forces come from outside the followers, or employees. Very little concern is afforded to the other person's desires and goals. In contrast, impelling leadership makes use of forces within the followers themselves and guides followers to want to do certain tasks." The impelling leader is aided by several points:

— People follow their own ideas best.

— A leader should lead people to decide for themselves.

— Human nature causes people to resist when anything happens that affects their work, unless they have a part in planning the change.

Emergency situations often necessitate the compelling leadership style. However, the security executive should use the impelling approach whenever possible. Because loss prevention programs are faced with numerous complex threats from a constantly changes world, the executive should solicit opinions from subordinates, many of whom may have good solution. Furthermore, managers should plant the seeds of ideas for change should keep subordinates thinking about alternative approaches to problems. Then, it is the quality leader who guides subordinates to clarify own creative solutions or one that was on the leader's mind originally, strategies are especially important when a workforce is subject to increased security. Since security is characterized by restricting freedom of movement (which is unpopular with the workforce), the astute security executive takes heed of impelling leadership and associated human relations strategies.

Theories of Leadership

Research on leadership has been approached from several perspective including style (just discussed), the situation, personality traits, and leader behaviour. Many theories exist, and newer approaches are unfolding all the time.

Managerial grid. This concept was developed by Robert R. Blake and Jane S. Mouton." It can be perceived as a theory to understand leadership styles. A manager's style is described on a two-dimensional model on which one axis is concern 'for production" and the other is "concern for people." Each axis ranges from low concern to high concern.

Controlling

Managerial control is a crucial function that monitors actual performance against plans. For the successful organization, planning and controlling are inseparable, especially since the workplace does not always operate smoothly. The sharp executive designs controls during the planning process so that when plans are implemented, they can be checked for compliance.

Many firms employ a controller (or comptroller) who manages the control function. In large corporations, this individual reports to the financial vicepresident or to the CEO. The controller makes use of financial records and analyses while managing the accounting process, including budgeting, for the purpose of protecting company assests. The loss prevention specialist can obviously be an aid to the controller.

An example of a major control function is auditing. It can be as simple as a patrolling security officer going through a checklist of physical security devices to verify operational effectiveness or as complex as internal auditors studying financial records at several corporate plants. Numerous other management controls exist. Accounting controls, such as separation of duties and job rotation, prevent financial loss by bookkeepers and accountants. Personnel performance appraisals act as a control over employee work behavior. Management information systems (MIS) are at the foundation of controls, since vital information is supplied to decision makers.

People who are in tune with contemporary management theories know the potential negative impact of controls on subordinates. The planning and implementation of controls is a delicate process that requires the utmost concern for positive human relations; otherwise, resentment may be generated as emotions intensify.

The Three-Step Control Process

Management theorists agree that the control process consists of three steps: (1) formulating standards of performance, (2) measuring performance against standards, and (3) taking corrective action.

Formulating Standards of Performance: Standards are similar to objectives. They are tuge that must be claerly stated and communicated.

Considerable controversy is being generated by those who favor security standards for various industries. This commendable effort will remain unresolved for years as the courts play a dominant role in establishing security standards by comparing similar organizations when a civil suit for negligent security targets a specific business. It is the job of the protection executive to look to emerging security guidelines and court decisions and to strive to establish such standards for his or her employer.

Standards of performance relate to personnel and to systems. A retail department store with a record of about twenty shoplifting apprehensions each Thanksgiving holiday should have a repeat performance each year unless conditions change. An investment in a CCTV system and card access a system should cut personnel costs while maintaining security.

Measuring Performance Against Standards: Information is the key to gauging actual performance against standards. Activities that produce concrete results (e.g., sales, arrests) provide easily available information. Performance results of research and development or crime prevention strategies, in contrast, may be difficult to measure.

If shoplifting apprehensions drop at a retail store, or if an investment in CCTV and a card access system reduces personnel costs but increases unauthorized entries, then performance is faltering. However, intervening variables must be considered. Apprehensions may drop if civil suit are increasing because of inadequate training and poor performance during apprehensions. An increase in unauthorized entries must be studied in light of a large onpremises construction project or an increase in customer traffic.

Taking Corrective Action: When performance falters, specific personnel must be in place with a appropriate authority and responsibility to facilitate corrections. An unexpected drop in shoplifting apprehensions or an increase in unauthorized entries requires investigation; such situations must be rectified. This is the final phase of control.

Management Controls

A prime objective of management controls is to ensure that business plans are fulfilled. Various management controls aim to prevent deviations in the quality and quantity of the resources used by an organization.

Human resources management, for example, attempts to control the quality and quantity of personnel. Personnel quality is controlled through job applicant screening, a major loss prevention strategy. Human resource planning should recruit the right number of personnel; too few employees restrict business plans, and too many employees hurt profits. Policy implementation and job descriptions are controls that aid this process.

Businesses must also control the quality of the materials that are converted into finished products; a sufficient invmxtcrrv is also required. Statistical sampling is used to control quality by inspecting samples rather than the entire lot. This approach is faulty, however, since such sampling may miss inferior materials. From a loss prevention standpoint, control this area is becoming an increasingly serious matter. Counterfeit or shoddy goods and raw materials are being dumped on numerous markets. Bogus items include assorted manufactured parts, clothes, and medical supplies to name a few. Obvious safety and lifethreatening problems result when unknowing organizations, customers, and patients are on the receiving and of these inferior goods. Purchasers must be aware of this problem. Corporations and government agencies have expanded their investigative efforts to ferret out unscrupulous business people who produce counterfeit goods. Also, consideration must be given to laws involving copyrights, trade secrets, patents, and trademarks.

Control also deals with the resource known as capital. From a business viewpoint, the acquisition of capital is controlled by the potential for profitability. Return on investment is a developing strategy for the prevention executives searching for improved budget justification. Security and loss prevention expenditures should be planned as an investment with a payback.

The analysis of investment proposals is a highly developed topic in to financial management." One example is the *payback* method—a simple, widely used approach that computes the number of years needed for a proposed capital acquisition to repay its original cost out of future cash earnings. To control security and loss prevention expenditures, upper management will increasingly demand that the protection executive demonstrate that the acquisition of capital for security systems will generate a profit.

Control of financial resources is accomplished through budgeting—a basic management tool to plan and control income and expenditures. Typically, in businesses, raw materials are purchased, finished products are manufactured, sales are made, and then cash is received. Cash must be controlled to pay expenses to further the business cycle. To aid this products are of controlling financial resourcesand as a way to check a business's "vital signs"—managers use ratios, such as the ratio of current assets to current liabilities. The minimum may be set at 2:1 and the maximum at 3:1; this recognizes the cost of both too little and too much investment in liquid assets.

Because a firm's accounting records and financial statements provide the foundation for business decisions, accuracy is important. The job of a certified public accountant (CPA) is to conduct an audit of a company's financial records to ensure that the records are dependable and credible. A favorable opinion by a CPA is expressed in an audit report. This is called the attest function. The security practitioner also plays a role in this control function to ensure the accuracv of financial records. He or she may have to assist management with controls to prevent embezzlement and fraud and may work with auditorsto investigate deviations. This is a major area wi losz, prevention.

Program Evaluation and Review Technique (PERT) This management tool was developed by the U.S. Navy during the 1950s to monitor the construction of submarines. A PERT chart is appropriate for projects in which several sequentially interdependent activities are planned. Major activities of a project are listed before a sequence of steps is prepared. Since certain steps require prerequisites, the order of activities must be carefully planned. As shown in Figure 64. an arrow indicates the allotted tinke between activities. During planning, the manager should compute tile critical path (the longest path) through the PERT network. This information can be used to note that any delay in this path will cause a delay in the whole project, whereas lag in another path may not be as damaging.

Although PERT was originally devised for large, complicated projects, it can be applied to a host of activities, such as switching from a manual to an automated system, conducting an investigation, or planning a convention. just about any project can be PERTcharted. This tool helps managers plan in detail and control work according to a timetable. Critical areas and problems are easier to pinpoint because of the visual nature of PERT.

Personnel Performance Appraisal

The basic purpose of an employee appraisal system is to measure work performance against a job description or previously prepared standards or objectives and then to work toward constructive correction of deficiencies. This evaluation process is an important management control function. Care must be exercised in the planning of evaluations to ensure that the system is legally and scientifically defensible:

Performance appraisal systems serve the following functions:

— Subordinates receive feedback on their performance.

— Productivity can be increased, as seen with an MBO program tied into an employee appraisal process.

— The promotion potential of subordinates is revealed.
— An equitable distribution of opportunities and rewards is facilitated.
— Performance appraisals provide direction for employee training and development programs.
— Prejudicial treatment of minorities is prevented.
— Results of evaluations are used in research. job applicant screening methods are validated by using evaluations as a measure of success.

Four major types of appraisal methods are MBO trait evaluation, global essays, and behaviorally anchored rating scales.

Trait evaluation, which is widely used, consists of rating subordinates on a group of traits. There are many trait evaluation instruments that cover such topics as job knowledge, ability to get along with others, trustworthiness, creativity, dependability, and so forth. Although criticism has been leveled at trait evaluation because. of subjective judgments by superiors, it does have merit.

Global essays have been in use for many years. Basically. a superior writes an unstructured, overall summary of the employee's work performance for a ceftan period of time. Critics argue that global essays are too subjective and that they hinge on the writing abilities ot the evaluator. Some employers use the global essay to supplement trait evaluations.

The behaviorally anchored rating scale (BARS) stresses the measurement of observable behavior (during critical incidents) directed at work objectives. Critical incidents are defined by experienced workers and are used to discriminate among levels of performance. A vertical scale is used to delineate performancefrom extremely effective to very ineffective. Critics argue that the BARS lacks sufficient research support. However, it has these advantages: subordinate participation in defining critical incidents reduces defensiveness during evaluations; emphasis is placed on job-specificbehavior; and training can become more precise, ecause beb~a~l incidEmts are known.

An aftemative to the BARS is the behavior observation scale (BOS). Here the evaluator rates the frequency of job-related behavior.

The legal requirements of a performance appraisal system are subject to standards similar to job applicant screening methods. EEOC guidelines state that performance appraisals must not be discriminatory. Job-relatedness is a key issue. Recommendations include the following:

— Performance appraisals must be based on an analysis of the job and

— Performance standards.

— Job performance standards must be clear and well defined. They should be behaviorally based so that observable actions can be recorded.

— Performance standards must be communicated to subordinates.

— As with other methods used for employment decisions, performance appraisals must be valid and reliable.

— Subordinates should have an opportunity for appeal if they disagree, with their performance evaluation.'

It has been noted that "the number of court cases involving alleged discrimination in performance appraisal is not as great as those invol ving personnel selection. But the number is growing, and that trend is likely to continue."

When a performance appraisal is presented to a subordinate, emphasis should be placed on improving performance. This positive approach is more beneficial than lengthy criticism. Suggestions for improvement can include specific guidelines that will be helpful to the employee, such as reduction of errors by 10 percent over the next evaluation period. Although the subordinate should receive some constructive criticism for shortcomings, most of the appraisal meeting should concentrate on reinforcing good work performance.

Discipline

Discipline is a universal control device in that it encourages desired behavior. Good discipline should be immediate (a delay can destroy the connection between the improper behavior and the punishment), should have had prior warnings (work guidelines must be firmly established), and should be impersonal (without bias).

The requirement for due process is growing in the workplace, and the result is responsible, fair, and consistent discipline. The employer's power to hire and fire with or without cause is weakening. Legislation and union contracts have promoted due processfor example, the presumption of innocence until proof is obtained, the right to be heard, and in certain cases, representation.

11
Organizing

Theories of Organization

The history of organization theory is marked by disagreement. One way to make sense of the numerous theories in the literature is to contrast the two major viewpoints: traditional and modern.

The Traditional Perspective

In essence, the traditional perspective emphasizes a closed system in which the environment is predictable and uncertainty from within can be averted through planning and strict control. A primary goal of the organization is economic efficiency.

Max Weber, a German sociologist writing at the turn of the century, was a key figure in shaping the traditional viewpoint. He coined the term bureaucracy, which, in theory, was to be the epitome of efficiency. It was characterized by a specific purpose, with the efforts of all organizational members directed toward that purpose. Weber stressed division of labour, whereby each employee always performed the same task and became an expert at it. Weber favoured clear and strict hierarchy of authority, with authority flowing down the pyramid. To make sure that employees behaved in an appropriate fashion, a framework of rules was necessary. Impersonality was another hallmark of Weber's bureaucracy; decisions about people were to be unemotional and objective.

As we know today, the term bureaucracy has negative connotations of "red tape" delays, and frustrations. Most organizations are characterized in some ways as bureaucracies, and bureaucratic characteristics can enhance organizational efficiency, provided that extremes do not become counter productive.

The rigidity of the traditional viewpoint became a constant target for those who saw that it did not work in all instances. The downward flow of authority was questioned. Theorists argued that a leader's authority is determined by his or her subordinates' willingness to comply.

Environmental uncertainties also led to criticism of rigid, closed structures. Newer theorists perceived organizations in new ways as an increasingly complex world emerged.

The Modern Perspective

The gist of the modern perspective is to view the organization as an open system that interacts with an uncertain world. Difficulty in predicting the future, and surprises, reinforces a constant need for organizational survival strategies.

In developing an open-system model, theorists have referred to an organization as a black box, and the model identifies what goes in and comes out. Inputs include capital, raw materials, and market information Outputs include goods and services and profits (or losses). Although er black box model does not describe the internal activities of an organization it does illustrate the ongoing interaction between the organization and environment.

By referring to organizational subsystems, we can take a look at what goes on inside the black box. The three major organizational subsystems are, the technical, boundary-spanning, and managerial subsystems. The technical subsystem, also called production, transforms raw materials into finished goods and services. It is dependent on other subsystems, job titles show the functions of those in the boundary-spanning subsystem. For instance, strategic business planners study the environment to overcome obstacles while searching for opportunities. Purchasing agents are responsible for the input of raw materials. Salespeople hustle to amass buyers. All these individuals are said to be at the outer boundary of the organization as they maintain close ties to the outside environment. The managerial subsystem functions to join all subsystems together toward an organized effort. This is accomplished through directing, coordinating, and controlling.

Many theories of organization are related in some way to the traditional and modern viewpoints. Over the years, theorists have modified these theories, added a new twist, or proposed new terms-all to give their readers a clearer understanding of organizations.

The Organization Chart

An organization chart visually represents the formal organization. Many of the basics of organization can be seen on such a chart. All organization charts have two dimensions: vertical hierarchy and horizontal specialization. The former establishes the chain of command. The latter involves division of labour.

The most popular form of organizational charting is the vertical chart which illustrates a hierarchy from top to bottom. The horizontal chart is a variation of the vertical chart and is read from left to right Proponents of the horizontal form claim that we read from left to right, so such a chart is logically designed. Another variation is the circular chart, which places the chief executive at the center of concentric circles representing layers of subordinates. Supporters see dynamic relationships portrayed best through concentric circles. Despite these variations, the vertical chart is still the most frequently used.

Top executives decide on the placement of the security and loss prevention department within the organization chart. One perspective is given by Richard J. Healy and Timothy J. Walsh in Principles of Security Management.' They favour placing the S&LP executive not more than there steps down from the chief executive officer. This provides a level in the hierarchy at which crucial support can be obtained. As noted frequently in the literature, without genuine senior management support, security and loss prevention do not have much chance for success.

It is interesting to note that many security writers, this one not excluded, place security departments higher in the hierarchy on organization charts than what is often seen in reality. Indeed, this is positive thinking, but numerous senior executives have different views; and business management textbooks, in particular, rarely if ever include security in organization charts. However, protection is still gaining momentum, as shown by increasing numbers of vice-presidents in charge of loss prevention. These professionals are proving their value to organization.

The design of an organization chart is also influenced by human relations and personalities. Management positions require considerable "people skills"—that is, the ability to get along with others. This is half the job. Although an organization chart, on paper, may be in the form of neat little boxes and perfectly straight lines, the reality of the situation is that top executives carefully consider who will occupy which position, and they often design organization charts and positions around personalities. It is much easier to change an organization than to change personalities.

The informal organization exposes the limitations of the organization chart. This is where informal ties exist among employees who disregard formal communication channels and chain of command rules. An intricate web of relationships exists, which at times makes a shambles of the formal chart. Employees on a pistol team who maintain strong ties to each other and establish an informal organization of their own serve as one, of many examples.

Factors that Influence Organizational Structure

Management theorists often study factors that influence organizational structure. These factors provide a foundation for understanding why enterprises are designed in certain ways. Both internal and external factors affect structure and have a bearing on protection programs. The astute security and loss prevention executive perceives these factors and responds to the needs of the entity.

Three major internal factors are (1) organizational size, (2) type of operations, and (3) personnel. The greater the number of people in an organization, the more the need for coordination and control requirements and a formal structure. As an organization increases the number of products and services offered, a more sophisticated structure with specializations is required. Organizational structure is also influenced by the types of personnel employed. Everyone responds differently to policies, procedures, and controls. Richard M. Hodgetts points out the following (paraphrased from' Management): Highly educated employees are inclined to work better under, a participatory style, whereby they can utilize their backgrounds to solve problems. Less educated employees feel more comfortable with a bureaucratic style. Younger workers raised in affluent conditions often present bureaucratic rules and are more productive in flexible organizations. Older employees accept workplace restrictions more readily.' To deal with a diversity of employees, management should develop a particular style for each department and make adjustments for control and autonomy. Efficiency and effectiveness improve when organizational and personnel needs coexist.

Two primary external factors influencing an organization's structure are (1) technology and (2) environmental stability. Although technology is used internally, its use is dictated by the external environment. If most companies in a certain industry employ the latest technology, firms without such technology may suffer. If a business is faced with a constantly changing environment, reliance on formalities may have to give way to teamwork and informal relationships, especially if the firm is "playing catchup" to survive.

What we are focusing on here is often referred to as the contingency approach to designing organizations. This amounts to situational thinking, whereby steps are taken to make the organization fit the demands of present conditions. Traditional bureaucratic reasoning is avoided to make way for the premise that there is no single best way to structure an organization. Contingency design involves managerial decisions to adapt the organization to the environment. A unique organizational design results.

Other external variables influence organizational structure. Competition is an external pressure whereby a price cut or a new product introduced by a competitor can force a business to re-evaluate its organizational structure. Government regulation is another variable that, for example, can cause a utility to plan carefully for rate increases by establishing a department for this purpose. A union will cause a company to form an industrial relations Department to handle negotiations and grievances. External needs of clients and customers can also mandate specific organizational structures.

Organizational Structures

The implications for security and loss prevention programs are not difficult to grasp. As stated in the earlier chapter on planning, protection efforts must respond to organizational needs. An R&D firm in a fiercely competitive business environment is likely to have an organic structure. Another example would be a retail chain that expands from five stores and one security persons to fifty stores and seventy security people in six years. An organic structure facilitates repeated in the overall organizational structure and the structure of the security department. The protection executive must understand that such a structure strengthens business survival and expansion in a rapidly changing world. Because security does not exist in a vacuum, becoming aware of internal and external forces helps the protection executive plan for constantly changing events. This reduces the stress of change and curbs surprises. Security and loss prevention departments should have the right combination of organic (to respond to changing business needs) and mechanistic (to maintain effective protection) structure.

Manufacturing organizations are often mechanistic in design since the objective is to produce goods as efficiently as possible. For a mature manufacturer in a stable and certain environment, protection would be less turbulent than it would be for an R&D firm.

Although certain businesses have either mechanistic or organic structures, many contain both. However, a mixture of structures can produce difficulty for management.

Paul R. Lawrence and Jay W. Lorsch, researchers from Harvard University who made a valuable contribution to contingency design theory, studied the relationship between two opposing structural forces and environmental complexity. One force, differentiation, is the tendency among specialists to think and act differently and for departments to develop certain philosophies concerning the external environment. Differentiation involves variations in management style, objectives, and timetables factors that fragment, an organization. Effective managers know how to obtain the right degree of, integration (the second opposing force), which is the collaboration among" specialists required to achieve a common purpose.'

Lawrence and Lorsch found that in successful firms, both differentiation and integration increased as environmental complexity increased. This applied not only to the overall organization but also to individual departments. Their research revealed that the more differentiated an organization, the more difficult it is to achieve integration.

The practical application of these views can lead to organizational failure in the face of environmental complexity if high differentiation and inadequate integration exist. These problems are compounded by specialists working at cross-purposes who are involved in "turf " conflicts. Integration can be achieved through policies and procedures, controls, cross-functional committees, liaison, and improved human relations.

The Lawrence and Lorsch research is applicable to the interdisciplinary nature of loss prevention. Several specialized departments within companies can assist loss prevention efforts—namely, risk management, legal, safety, fire protection, auditing, and information resource management. When these different departments go their separate without collaboration, this in itself is a loss or waste of resources major aim of this book is to help the practitioner understand, locate, utilize specialists who hold answers to protection problems.

The Matrix Organization

Matrix, also referred to as project management, is an organizational structure in which vertical and horizontal lines of authority are combined and the flow of authority is both down and across. This approach is appropriate large projects new product development, and complex problems. Mechanistic bureaucracies and demanding technical specifications forced managers to find a new way to work on huge projects. The organic approach led to the matrix format. Basically, a project manager borrows specialists from line m anagers who are over the engineering, manufacturing, and contract administration functions.

Coordination is the primary benefit of the matrix design. The project manager manages a project that would otherwise be fragmented among functional units. Increased coordination enhances control over personnel and costs. Flexibility permits specialists to be shifted among projects as needed.

The most obvious disadvantage of the matrix design is its violation of unity of command. Loyalty to one's own department can hinder effectiveness. Problems also arise because project managers lack formal line authority, and their authority is often less than their responsibility. Human relations skills are a prime avent, for the, project manager to get the job done.

Despite its pitfalls, the matrix organization is not a passing fad. Some of the largest corporations-such as General Electric, Citibank, Bechtel, and Dow Chemical consider the matrix design beneficial. Its use is growing, and most large organizations employ matrix structure for at least some period of time.

Although a matrix design, and for that matter other organizational structures, may be of little use to a protection executive, a knowledge of underlying theory as well as advantages and disadvantages provides useful information to aid investigations and for planning security. For example, if crime were occurring in a project coordinated via a matrix design, the investigator would gather information in not just one department, but several. A web of interrelations would require investigation, since the matrix design incorporates vertical and horizontal lines of authority. The planning of an information protection program for a project operating in a matrix fashion would likewise encounter unfamiliar lines of authority and complications.

Departmentalization

As we know, differentiation tends to fragment an organization, and various~ forms of integration must be introduced for coordination. Departmentlization, often the first step in designing an organization, is one form integration whereby related jobs and activities are grouped into major units.

Many S&LP departments begin as one-person operations in which: practitioner handles physical security decisions, in-house security awareness, investigations, and so forth. As the role of protection increases, so does the number of personnel in the department. Security officers, investigators, technicians, and other specialists are hired. Departmentalization becomes necessary because of the specialization and organizational complexity that accompanies growth. Various types of departmentalization exist. In practice, the needs of the organization dictate usage.

Functional departmentalization is the arrangement of a company around key activities (e.g., manufacturing sales, finance). Personnel are organized according to job function. Derivative departments can be created when activities increase. All major units report to a chief executive officer (CEO). Functional departmentalization is popular and easy to understand and employ.

Geographic departmentalization puts personnel "closer to the action" when a company has nationwide or worldwide business. A retail marketing manager would be in a better position to judge customer needs in southern California by working from a Los Angeles office rather than from corporate headquarters in New York City. In such a structure, regional security managers are assigned to investigate and correct problems in a specific geographic location. This regional position is responsible for several districts, covering multiple locations, and each district is handled by a subordinate. Such positions entail considerable travel. In the past, more than today, communications has been a problem because, geographically dispersed operations. With presentday telecommunications this problem is diminishing.

Departmentalization can also be categorized according to product or service, customer, and equipment or process. Companies with diversified product lines often create managerial units based on specific products. Or companies may organize around particular customer needs. The process or equipment used in production is another basis for departmentalization for example, all lathes located in one department. The security industry employs examples of departmentalization: contract security officers, investfirms are organized around services personnel protection programs are aimed at specific customers.

Span of Management

Following decisions on departmentalization, the next structural question concerns how many subordinates should be placed under the direction of one superior. This has been called span of control or span of supervision. Since we are emphasizing the activities of managers in this book, the term Span of management will be used. Some scholars favour this term, since managers do more than just "control"; they also plan, budget, organize, and so on.

Organizational leaders and researchers have been focusing on span of management for centuries. Napoleon stated that "no man can command more than five distinct bodies in the same theatre of war." Lyndall Urwick and V. A. Graicunas, often quoted in management literature, espouse this principle: "No executive should attempt to supervise directly the work of more than five, or at most six, direct subordinates whose work interlocks."' 1 Urwick stressed that the principle was not meant to apply at the lowest level of supervision, especially where the work of subordinates does not interlock.

Graicunas made an interesting contribution through his quantification of relationships between superiors and subordinates and between subordinates themselves. He pointed out that interactions increase substantially as subordinates are added. When a manager has two subordinates who interact with one another, six relationships exist: the manager relating to each subordinate as an individual; the manager relating to each subordinate, where each is a group member; and the interaction between the subordinates, as seen from the perspective of the two. The addition of a third subordinate increases the number of relationships to eighteen. A manager with eight subordinates would deal with 1,080 potential relationships. Graicunas proposed the following formula to determine the number of relationships.

Let as use subordinates to illustrate the formula:

$r = 8(2^8 - 1 + 8 - 1)$
$r = 8\ (2^7 + 7)$
$r = 8(128 + 7)$
$r = 8(135)$
$r = 1{,}080$ potential relationships

A survey of the span of management literature reveals that spans vary greatly and are based upon several variables:

— The complexity of subordinates' jobs and need for guidance complex investigations often require close supervision)

— The complexity of manager's job (e.g., a very busy manager should have a narrow span of management)

— The number of people with whom the manager and subordinates must interact

— The extent of support provided to superiors and subordinates assistants, control techniques and equipment, computers)

— The competence of personnel

— Administrative costs

— Productivity

— Job satisfaction

Overly narrow and overly wide spans are counterproductive, former have been criticized for causing tall organizations, characterized by, oversupervision, lengthy lines of communications, multilevel decision making, and increased costs. Overly wide spans can erode efficiency cause both interpersonal and coordination problems. An ideal span exist. Research has produced support for both narrow and wide management: "Future research must clearly identify not only the which may affect the span, but also the criteria upon which a judgements of 'too large' or 'too small' are to be based.""

Centralization and Decentralization

The key point here involves upper management's decisions on retaining or delegating authority, in highly centralized organizations, top management dominates decision making. Decentralization is characterized by an increase in lower-level decision making.

Those in favour of decentralization claim that middle and lower-level managers are capable of increased decision making authority with less delay. People closest to a problem are generally familiar with complex factors that provide a foundation for decisions. Decentralization also creates a competitive environment among units, allows for the development of personnel, and produces greater job satisfaction and productivity. Top executives' time can be better utilized when they do not have to become involved in day-to-day decisions; more time can be spent on strategic planning and on the future of the business.

Decentralization can present difficult security problems. With multiple locations, sometimes in the hundreds, businesses have to make decisions on the most appropriate form of protection. Policies and procedures must be prepared and communicated successfully. A national retailer, for example, may have store, district, and regional security managers as a control measure.

Opponents argue that the control function is handicapped through decentralization. Senior managers typically want to know precisely what i occurring throughout an organization on a daily basis, instead of waiting periodic reports. A constant flow of information enables correct made quickly, rather than after periodic reports arrive and a gotten worse. Centralization enhances coordination and reduces of effort. Decisions are more consistent, and disagreements are strong central leadership.

Strong arguments can be made in favour of centralizing security grams. In certain companies, placing security under local management control borders on the absurd. Serious problems may never be reported to corporate headquarters, and investigations may be quashed. The executive in charge of corporate security should have the authority to direct and control all phases of protection. This includes investigations and the selection and inspection of security contracts and systems. Decentralization must be carefully controlled with an eye toward potential vulnerabilities.

Confidentiality of information can be better maintained if only a few centralized executives are privy to such information. This is especially important for high-technology firms and for other businesses facing fierce competition.

Generally, centralization works well in stable organizations that are dealing with a stable environment. Decentralization seems to be a wise choice when an organization has to deal with quickly changing conditions. Organizations often use both. As with other management strategies there is no one correct way of centralizing or decentralizing authority. Numerous variables must be considered, such as the size of the organization, the types of technology available for organizational tasks, the knowledge and skills of subordinates, the time frame for decisions, and controls.

Delegation

Decentralization depends on effective delegation of authority, which can be defined as the process of assigning specific decision-making power to subordinates. Although a superior may delegate authority to a subordinate, responsibility ultimately rests with the superior. A famous illustration of this principle is noted by the sign former president Harry S. Truman had on his desk: "The Buck Stops Here!" A security manager who delegates the investigation of internal theft to a subordinate will hold that assistant accountable for successful case resolution, but the security manager is ultimately responsible if prosecution fails and civil action follows.

Managers may refrain from delegating authority for numerous reasons limited confidence in subordinates, inadequate management controls, fear of competition from subordinates, and belief in the fallacy "If you want it done right, do it yourself." The manager who does not delegate when such opportunities exist is making a serious mistake. Having an overwhelming number of tasks can reduce the effectiveness of a manager and can produce excessive stress. Failure to delegate is a major reason behind poor performance by managers.

Delegation has three specific benefits: it allows managers to have more time for important management functions, such as planning and control; it is a valuable training and development tool; and it can satisfy subordinates desire for challenges.

Authority and Power

Authority is the right to act. It involves directing subordinates to pursue organizational objectives. People in organizations generate authority the top down and from the bottom up. The topdown perspective is reflected in the classical view, whereby authority originates from the world outside and the organization grants managers formal authority to do their Jobs.

This classical perspective should be viewed idealistically. If every subordinate adhered to its premise, orders would be followed without much problem, and discipline problems would diminish.

The bottomup view helps to explain why subordinates selectively resist orders. Here, authority evolves from below; if subordinates see an order as legitimate, it will be followed. Without legitimacy, orders are disobeyed. Rewards and punishment are the ageless tools to deal with subordinate resistance.

To be effective, managers need authority from above and below. Leadership skills and the development of clout characterize managers who generate followers.

Organizational power is reflected in an individual's ability to obtain resources to reach certain objectives." Whereas authority is the right to act, power is the ability to act. One source of power stems from an individual's position. Control of information, the formulation of policies, and the distribution of rewards are some of the ways in which power can be exercised. A leader also obtains power from within through specialized knowledge and personality characteristics. Another source of power develops when a subunit of an organization increases its influence because of the circumstances at hand. Falling sales could cause a marketing executive to gain power as management looks to this executive for answers. Serious lawsuits against a corporation could cause the legal department to become the focus of attention and power. Likewise, the security and loss prevention executive can gain power if an organization requires a specific type of protection for survival.

Organizational Politics

Authority and power are intertwined with organizational politics. Executives often engage in political behaviour to elevate their authority and power. Organizational politics can be defined as the process of increasing one's influence and power over others and over resources through the use of informal strategies.

The political environment in our society is characterized by interest groups vying for power and scarce resources. Each group attempts to promote itself while discrediting the opposition. Similarly, in corporations, coalitions of interest groups compete with each other.

Organizational politics is a fact of life. Power-oriented executives thrive on political excitement while reviewing "what if " scenarios and political tactics in their minds. This behaviour is an essential part of how strong leaders omerge. Ethical and legal considerations surface when political behaviour and tactics become questionable.

The range of political tactics is limited by one's imagination, besides ethical and legal constraints. To begin with, a power-oriented executive must build a power base of flowerers. This can be accomplished when two or more departments are interdependent. For example, security, safety, fire protection and risk management have ties to each other.

"Log rolling" is another tactic whereby an exchange of favours occurs. It is similar to the legislative practice of "log rolling" or "mutual back scratching." By exchanging favours with a more powerful person, one's opportunities are enhanced.

Beginning something on a small scale with the potential for growth is another tactic of the shrewd executive. A topnotch salesperson who conducts his or her own marketing studies may be producing the seeds for a marketing department. The protection executive has many avenues for growthfor example, successfully investigating a few workers' compensation cases and then capturing the whole program after showing senior management a commendable return on investment; handling some risk management functions, which illustrates competence to take on more such responsibilities.

Committees

Some people thrive on committee meetings and enjoy attending more than they can fit into their schedule. Others view these gatherings negatively and describe them in words inappropriate for this book. "Oh no, not another committee" is often echoed in organizations. Boredom and sleepiness pervasively afflict many committee members. Nevertheless, many committees perform useful functions by cutting across formal lines of authority and departmentalization.

Organizations often establish standing, committees, which are permanent groups assigned specific responsibilities. Ad hoc committees are temporary groups formed for a specific problem. Several other types of committees exist, and usage varies.

"Two heads are better than one"' is a major premise behind committees. Decisions that require considerable interdisciplinary expertise benefit from a group effort. An organization readying a skyscraper to become a "smart building" where energy, HACV, access control, CCTV, and emergency procedures are being planned would benefit from a committee composed of engineers, architects, and safety and security specialists. A community college planning to construct new parking lots and modify existing parking regulations should seek input from a cross section of the college community.

Salary expenses are wasted on committees when there are too many members, when inappropriate members are assigned, and when certain members waste time by talking about irrelevant topics.

Groupthink is a problem whereby group members develop an illusion of invulnerability, leading to excessive optimism and collective rationalizations. This is a particular danger for security programs, although the writings on this subject have focused on the federal government-specifically, the failed Bay of Pigs invasion and decisions prior to the attack on Pearl Harbor.

Emotional and attitudinal factors within a committee-as well as questioning, debating, and conflict-can reach unhealthy levels, thereby causing frustration for members. When a committee receives poor results, it is difficult to hold members accountable. Each may blame the others.

The benefits of committees outweigh the disadvantages. Executives must take charge and set guidelines for committees so that human resources are not wasted. Member selection, committee size, a well-planned agenda, quality leadership, and open-mindedness are all important.

12

The Scope of Security and Loss Prevention

Security and Loss Prevention Defined

Many definitions have evolved for the word security. Here, it will be narrowly defined as traditional methods (guards, fences, alarms) used to increase the likelihood of a crime-controlled, tranquil, and noninterupted environment for an individual or organization in pursuit of objectives.

Loss prevention originated from the insurance industry as a way to reduce losses and premiums through, for example, fire-resistive construction materials. It is a much broader term than security. Practitioners in the security and loss prevention field, faced with an increasingly complex world and formidable loss problems, must expand their horizons in a search for solutions. Loss prevention taps numerous disciplines for ideas. Loss prevention is broadly defined as a wide variety of methods used by an individual or organization to increase the likelihood of averting losses. The methods include not only traditional security strategies be counter-measures developed from business, auditing, data processing, risk management, fire protection, safety, engineering, architecture, psychology, sociology, and other disciplines. Loss prevention is thus an interdisciplinary approach to the problem of loss.

Losses

Executives who are responsible for security and loss prevention often concentrate on crimes, fires, and accidents. Contemporary practitioners also look beyond traditional, serious threats to other sources of loss, such as substance abuse in the workplace, terrorism, and environmental damage. When we consider the resultant harm and the costs of counter-measures for these occurrences, we are dealing with billion-dollar problems.

An accurate description of losses must consider both direct and indirect losses. Direct losses are immediate and obvious. Indirect losses are prolonged and often hidden. A robbery and murder at a supermarket results in direct losses from the death of a person and lost money. Indirect losses from such an occurrence are the psychological impact on store employees, possible increases in insurance premiums, and concerned customers' switching to a competitor. When such complex problems as internal theft or substance abuse in the workplace are considered, total direct and indirect losses are staggering.

The Development of Security and Loss Prevention

To confront so many sources of loss, several strategies have developed throughout history. Public police and private security forces in the United States have a strong English heritage. In 1748, the English magistrate Henry Fielding developed the idea of preventing crime through police action. He wrote about and advocated the need for well-paid men to patrol the highways plus separate units called "runners," to move quickly to the scenes of crimes to investigate. As the Industrial Revolution gained momentum, urban problems grew worse. Citizens and businessmen increasingly hired private police for protection, since the public police around London Nvere fragmented and limited in their effectiveness. The eighteenth and nineteenth centuries were difficult times; urban slums grew, and men, women, and children worked up to sixteen hours a day. At one time, 160 crimes were punishable by hanging, including stealing a loaf of bread.'

The chaos of urban crime in England led to a revolution in policing known as the Peelian reform movement. In 1829, Sir Robert Peel introduced into Parliament the Metropolitan Police Act, and policing as we known it today began. The Peelian reform principles include the following, which an still applicable today in both the public and private sectors.

- The securing and training of proper persons is at the root of efficiency.
- Good appearance commands respect.
- The deployment of police strength, both by time and area, is essential.
- No quality is more indispensable to a policeman than a perfect command of temper. A quiet, determined manner has more effect than violent action.

Although Peelian reforms did much to professionalize the police and curb urban crime, private police were still in demand. During this time, the United States saw the need for organized police departments to replace the watchmen who walked the streets. Many of Peel's ideas were brought to America to assist in the establishment of urban police forces. And, England, private security was still being sought for protection. During middle of the nineteenth century, security companies expanded considerably in the United States, with banks, railroads, and the U.S. Army as major clients. For example:

1855—Allan Pinkerton began the famous security

service agency, providing a full range of protection and investigative offerings.

1858—Edwin Holmes established the first central station alarm system.

1891—Washington Perry Brink began providing an armored car service.

1909—William J. Burns began his detective agency.

As the protection needs of the business community increased, so did the range of services, geographic expansion, and profits of these security companies. These names still exist today among the giants of the private security industry.

World War 11 played a great role in stimulating the growth of the private security industry. Before national defense contracts could be awarded, the federal government required that contractors establish strict security measures at to protect classified materials and defense secrets. Management at industrial plants became more aware of the need for security to protect personnel, assets, and proprietary information.

The history of loss prevention can be traced to the latter part of the nineteenth century. At that time, insurers began to focus greater attention on the problem of primarily wooden construction in urban areas and the devastating fires that occurred. Extensive fire losses resulted in higher insurance premiums, which made insurance economically unfeasible for many. The insurers and the insured faced hardship, Something had to be done to reduce losses and premiums while preserving the insurance industries. After the Civil War, fire insurance companies formed the National Board of Fire Underwriters, which utilized the specializations of engineering, investigation, research, and education to prevent losses. Improved building construction and the use of fire-resistive materials grew as loss prevention strategies. Today, loss prevention is a major part of the insurance industry. It has also spread to corporate America as a way to reduce premiums, protect assets, and promote business survival. Many security, safety, and fire protection professionals, as well as upper management, are turning to loss prevention for possible answers to their problems.

Which Strategies are Best to Counter Losses?

One primary and practical way to understand the security, and loss prevention field is to study the loss problems facing organizations and the resultant countermeasures. Losses from crimes, fires, accidents, natural disasters, and so forth, are the obvious problems. The strategies to counter these losses are numerous. A reader with even the slightest knowledge can list the more common ones: security officers, alarm systems, planning and preparation, and the like. It is of the utmost importance, however, for practitioners to look beyond these basic strategies to new methods. A never-ending search for new and better ideas is a necessity in dealing with our complex, changing world. A major purpose of this book is to present a management foundation for the development and implementation of state-of-theart loss prevention methods. Research is an integral part of this process, especially since certain S&LP strategies are simply not working and others exist simply because they have been in operation for years and nobody has questioned them. Furthermore, unnecessary or inappropriate security equipment is acquired by those without the time, resources, or expertise to make sound purchasing decisions. What we have in our field are many good questions but a shortage of well-researched and tested answers. Subsequent chapters will answer some of these questions, but more important are the skills and the critical thinking perspective the reader should acquire to assist in answering future questions so that the best possible loss prevention strategies can be implemented.

Public-and Private-Sector Strategies

The public and private sectors have intertwined roles in dealing with a host of loss problems, whether they be crimes, fires, or accidents.

Four basic factors differentiate public and private-sector police. The generalizations have exceptions, however. For example, to save money, government agencies are increasingly establishing contracts with private-sector service companies for public safety and security needs. Another exception is seen when public police, fire, and safety personnel visit businesses to expose loss vulnerabilities and recommend corrective action. Whereas the private sector emphasizes prevention while limiting arrests, public policewho are arrest oriented have become more aware of the importance of prevention.

Contract versus Proprietary Programs

The establishment of security and loss prevention programs in businesses usually takes one of two forms: contract or proprietary. Many businesses save money by contracting the work. Others view a proprietary or in-house program as the best because they can maintain total control without having to deal with outsiders. Still other organizations favour a combination of the two forms as the best choice.

Some arguments advanced over the years claim that contract services are more flexible in terms of personnel required, have lower costs, and reduce the time that management has to devote to personnel screening, supervision, training, and providing uniforms and equipment. Employee quality and turnover are the greatest disadvantages of contract services. Proprietary protection programs afford considerable control over many areas, including quality of personnel, supervision, specialized training, and satisfying specific industry needs. Higher cost is the prime disadvantage of a proprietary program.

Many executives believe that contract protection is by far the best avenue. Others have a completely opposite view and support it with strong arguments. The debate will surely continue, but the choice is best made by studying the unique needs of a particular organization.

Security and Loss Prevention Research

One major area that has consistently hindered the effectiveness of security and loss prevention is the lack of supportive research. This weakness is being corrected slowly, as more and more questions and problems are being brought to the surface. For those interested in research, this field is ripe; practitioners want quality answers.

Three major national studies (funded by the federal government) of the private security industry are summarized here. It should be emphasized that these three studies focused on private security. Perhaps future studies will stress loss prevention (i.e., security, safety, and fire protection). Such research, known as a "Cost-of-Risk Survey," has been completed by a joint effort of the Risk and Insurance Management Society (RIMS) and the Risk Planning Group, Darien, Connecticut.

The Rand Repor

The first major study to focus solely on private security was done for the U.S. Department of justice by the Rand Corporation in 1972. This report emphasized the problems and needs of the private security industry.

Although exposure of the extensiveness of private security surprised many, the report was not received well by the industry because inadequate training and abuses of authority were brought to national attention. Furthermore, the industry was depicted as "policing-for-profit" to meet the needs of special-interest groups. Licensing of security businesses and registration of personnel were among the suggested guidelines for the future.

One often-cited statement from this report was that "the typical private guard is an while male, poorly educated, usually untrained, and very poorly paid. Much criticism has been leveled at this statement, and as later national study, the typical security officer has changed over the years.

The Report of the Task Force on Private Security

The justice Department's Task Force on Private Security undertook what was touted as the first national effort to set standards and goals to maximize the effectiveness and competency of the private security industry. The task force's report stressed the importance of the licensing of security service businesses and the registration of personnel.' Emphasis was placed on establishing uniform standards for selection and training of personnel, improving public-private police cooperation, reinforcing a code of ethics, and the need for research on a wide variety of topics. Two major objectives were to curb industry abuses while promoting professionalism. Private security was also identified as a massive and underutilized resource.

The Halicrest Report

In 1985, the National Institute of justice, successor to the Law Enforcement Assistance Administration, published Private Security 'and Police in America: The Hallcrest

Report. The National Institute of Justice had contracted with Hallcrest Systems, Inc. to research specific questions on the private security industry:

1. What are the roles and contributions of private security and public law enforcement in crime control?
2. How do the public and private sectors view each other?
3. What is the status of their communications and cooperation?
4. What are the characteristics of the private security industry?

One key result of the Hallcrest report is evidence that the industry has improved since the Rand and justice Department task force reports were published. This change can be seen, for instance, in the typical security officer of today, who is more likely to be younger (31 to 35 years of age) and more likely (50 percent) to have completed some college-level work.

The Hallcrest report noted that annual expenditures for private security are estimated at $22 billion, while $14 billion is spent on federal, state, and local law enforcement agencies. Total U.S, employment in private security is about 1.1 million, excluding federal security workers. The ratio of private police to public police is nearly 2:1, and this disparity is likely to grow.'

Industry Problems and Recommendations

Several problems characterize the private security industry. It is important for people connected to this industry to develop an understanding of these problems so that they can begin to work toward solutions.

Public Police and Secondary Employment

The Hallcrest Report highlighted moonlighting by public police in the private security industry as a problem area. The following observations were noted in the report :

— Public police working in the private sector often use their departmental uniforms and equipment.

— Twenty-four percent of police personnel were engaged in off-duty security employment.

— Approximately 150,000 local law enforcement officers are regularly engaged in off-duty private security employment in the United States. Police executives view certain types of security work performed by police as a conflict of interest. Examples are off-duty police involvement as security contractors and police unions engaged in obtaining security employment for their members. A detective moonlighting as a private investigator could compromise departmental information. A patrol officer could provide differential response to those who pay for private security services performed by off-duty police.

— Liability is another concern. Once a police officer acts, it is generally not relevant whether the officer was on or off duty, in uniform or plain-clothes, or even employed in private security. A police department may be held liable for the officer's actions, as well as for disability claims if the officer is injured. One solution attempted by police executives is to obtain third-party waiver of liablity from the officer and the off-duty employer.

— Concern about officers' fitness for duty after long hours of moonlighting has prompted police executives to place a limit of twenty hours on off-duty employment per week.

False Alarms

The false alarm problem has plagued the security industry for years and has been a cause of friction between public and private police. Even the term false alarm is subject to considerable debate. In a common scenario, public police arrive at the scene of an alarm, but no break-in or intruder can be found. At this point, the police often assume that the alarm was false and blame it on user error or some type of malfunction. However, other explanations are possible: A burglar could have been frightened away by the alarm or approaching police. The alarm may have modified authorities about an unsecured door Although it is widely believed that over 95 percent of alarm activations are false, the percentage of these activations that perform a preventive function is difficult to gauge. Perhaps a new term, such as unexplained alarm is needed.'

The Hallcrest report stated the following in reference to the false problem.

— Ten to 12 percent of all public police calls-for-service were for false alarms.

— In Houston, for example, an estimated 70,000 alarm systems produced 78,652 false alarms in 1982, taking up 15 percent of police time at a cost of $7 million.

— The alarm-response work-load on public police continues to grow.

— Fifty-seven percent of public police executives in the Hallcrest research favoured transferring burglar alarm response to the private sector.

— Alarm control ordinances can reduce the false alarm problem. Locations that have too many false alarms are required to pay a penalty fee to the local government.

— Ordinances with a permit system are advantageous. For example, in Miami, police will not respond to an alarm from premises without a permit or if the owner has not paid earlier fines. This has resulted in lower police costs and a drop in the number of calls. Baseline data help to evaluate the permit system while providing information on which locations or systems create the most false alarms.

Public and Private Police Relationships

Public police frequently have a low opinion of private security officers. Contract security is characterized by low pay, inadequate screening, limited training, and high turnover, and comparison with public police services shows wide differences. Even the general public has a stereotypical of images private security officers. Readers are probably familiar with the term "rent-a-cop" the derogatory name used pervasively to describe private security officers. What users of this term may not realize is that there are thousands of security officers who have better qualifications than the average police officer.

The Hallcrest report noted the following:

— Public police executives and officers were asked to rate the performance of private security. Overall, they gave private security a fair-to-poor rating in most areas.

— It is interesting that when security managers were asked how they were rated by public police, their perception proved to be more critical than reality, suggesting a negative self-image on the part of contract security, officers and, to a lesser extent, proprietary security officers.

— Hallcrest research ~showed that the impact of private security on the overall safety and security of communities has not been fully recognized by public police.

— Public and private police made the following recommendations for improving the quality of private security:
  - — Improve training,
  - — Improve personnel selection methods,
  - — Pay higher wages, and
  - — Establish and improve licensing and regulation.

— The following recommendations were made for improving public and private sector relations:
  - — Closer cooperation,
  - — Management meetings,
  - — Understanding respective roles,
  - — Information exchange, and
  - — Improving communication.

Private Justice

Generally, public police are arrest-oriented. Private police stress prevention and deemphasize arrests. Since businesses exist to make a profit, management often perceives involvement with the criminal justice system as not cost-effective. Public police who make a career change to private security must prepare themselves for these differences in organizational objectives. Private justice basically involves internal action by a business to deal with employee dishonesty." Management options include suspension without pay, dismissal, transfer, or mandatory restitution. Private justice views involvement of the criminal jusiice system as a poor choice for the following reasons:

— Prosecution is an inconvenience, especially if lengthy court proceedings ensue.

— Prosecution expenses would entail personnel and legal costs. A civil suit might result.

— By not prosecuting, the company may salvage a valuable, experienced employee in whom it has invested training dollars.

— Bad publicity for the company might result.

— Insurance premiums may rise.

— Strong arguments can be made by those favouring prosecution:

— Prosecution sets an example that might deter future offenses.

— The business would rid itself of an employee-offender who may have committed previous offenses and may commit future ones.

— A strong prosecution policy would become known inside and outside the business. This might deter offenders from seeking employment with the business.

According to the Hallcrest report: "Some observers have expressed concern that private justice may exert far greater control on citizens than the criminal justice system itself, and in the process may ignore basic principles of law and "airness." Before establishing security policies, business executives should study all variables and potential results. "Further research in this area would help delineate the characteristics of private justice, its contribution to reducing the work-load of the criminal justice system, and the amount of under-reported crime which accompanies its use.

The Hallcrest report stated the following findings:

— The crimes most frequently reported to police are burglary, robbery, arson, cargo theft, extortion, receiving stolen property, and terroism and bombings.

— The least frequently reported crimes are pilferage and employee theft, insurance fraud, industrial espionage, commercial bribery and computer-related crimes. Nearly half the security managers reported resolving employee theft incidents within the organization.

— Public police may not have the expertise to handle certain crimes.

— Companies often make a simple economic decision, forgoing prosecutJon in order to avoid increases in insurance or deciding that losses are more easily recovered by raising prices to the consumer.

— Civil suits are a major way that companies can recover damage from theft of proprietary information.

Halicrest Report Recommendations

The Hallcrest report espoused numerous recommendations, including following:

— Because "there is little cooperation between law enforcement and private security in crime prevention programs," these two should work together to promote public awareness and self-help sectors measures that could offset demands for some police services.

— Law enforcement agencies should appoint a high-ranking officer to act as liaison officer with private security managers.

— Public police should be involved in the design of security during the planning of new buildings and developments. Private security and police services should be integrated in large developments. Special taxing districts may be appropriate where special levels of police services are desired.

— "A federal tax credit for security expenditures, similar to the energy tax credit, might be a cost-effective way to reduce police work-loads."

— An assessment should be made of which public police services might be performed at lower cost by the Private sector.

— A non-profit economic crime institute should be established, with federal and private funding, to research economic crime and its impact on the gross national product and to promote awareness of this problem.

— "A non-profit Private Security Research Institute, financed by government and private sources, would be useful to monitor growth and trends in private protection resources and technology, and perhaps to develop security standards, strategies, technologies, evaluation techniques, and cooperative programs."

— "Statewide licensing should be required for guard and patrol, private investigation, and alarm firms."

— Minimum levels of training should be required for all security personnel and alarm technicians.

Security and Loss Prevention Management

Management's Perception of Security

The role that security plays in an organization depends primarily on management philosophy. On one end of the spectrum are those companies that tolerate security as a necessary nuisance that helps to reduce insurance premiums. Minimum support is geared to satisfy the insurer. A nonprofessional, "company cop" image is promoted, and security is relegated to an insignificant part of the organization, making its presence powerless. Losses are routinely passed on to customers. Security and loss prevention practitioners are often placed in a "now-in" situation. They are perceived as needlessly "crying" when they present warnings about impending disasters and the need for additional expenditures and precautions. But when chaos does strike, they are criticized for not providing enough warning and protection.

On the opposite end of the spectrum are those businesses that view security as an integral part of the management team. Risks, losses, and business survival are prime concerns. Security and loss prevention practitioners are seen as professionals who can contribute to the welfare and profits of the business.

Changing an overall negative management view of security can be a monumental task. Sometimes only a serious, expensive loss will spur management into focusing attention on the value of security expertise.

Whether the practitioner is attempting to alter management's negative view or strengthen a positive view, one important avenue is to prove that security is a profit center. This can be done by showing that money invested security has a return on investment—for example, savings in personnel costs by the purchase of a closed-circuit television system or hiring a bad-check~ specialist who recovers several times his or her salary. Only the practitioner's imagination limits the strategies. When security and loss prevention are explained in financial terms, management becomes more receptive.

The Direction of Modern S&LP Management

The enlightened security and loss prevention executive of today should strive to become a business person who specializes in S&LP. Although many S&LP practitioners have a law enforcement, criminal justice, or military background, the importance of accounting, auditing, business law, and risk management cannot be overstated. Other are-as-such as data processing, investment management, marketing, human relations, and stress management are also valuable. The S&LP profession is truly interdisciplinary, and, practitioners should be involved in perpetual study. This does not mean that the practitioner must be an expert in all disciplines.

Many such questions are being directed at our profession. The questions are demanding, but the answers are within our grasp. This book provides direction for responding to these questions and others, while promoting the development of the modem security and loss prevention executive.

Management Theory

Management can be defined as the process by which resources (i.e., people, money, machines, material) 'are 'coordinated to achieve specific goals. Viewpoints on the most advantageous ways to manage are constantly being advanced. One strategy may emphasize achieving goals through people, while another may stress the technical aspects of management. There is no general theory of management that serves to consolidate and direct researchers and practitioners. Because of great differences of opinion, the situation has been referred to as a jungle of approaches to management theory." The field is far from settled, and theorists argue that a general theory of management must be developed if the field is to take its place alongside other scientific disciplines.

To simplify this confusion, and to deemphasize management fads, we will discuss three major views on management to provide a foundation for the reader. Each theory is summarized here, and elaborations are given in other sections of this book as the older and newer approaches to management are explained.

Management Science: The father of management science is Frederick Taylor (1856-1915), who was one of the first efficiency engineers. In the early part of this century, he argued that workers, not machines, were the cause of inefficiency. His research coined the terms time study, work planning, and fatigue study. The results of his studies showed that workers could carry nearly four times more iron each day if they received periodic rests; thus the coffee break arrived in the workplace. Taylor stressed that efficiency and productivity could be improved through definite work assignments, rules, and close supervision.

Frank B. (1868-1924) and Lillian M. (1878-1972) Gilbreth were two other contributors to management science. They studied worker efficiency and devised a "speed work" system whereby wasted efforts by workers were eliminated. Precise work performance guidelines were designed, published, and used by industrial engineers. The book and movie Cheaper by the Dozen evolved from this husband-and-wife team, who applied their specialization to their home life with twelve children.

The Management Cycle: In contrast to Taylor and the Gilbreths, Henri Fayol (1841-1925), a French engineer, studied management itself. He was the first to propose a series of "principles of management," which provide guideposts for successful management. These principles included centralization, authority, discipline, and esprit de corps-terms we are all accustomed to today. Fayol also developed a management cycle that continuously repeats itself as managers do their job: (1) planning, (2) organizing, (3) commanding, (4) coordinating, and (5) controlling.

Behavioral Science: The efforts of scientific management to humanize to humanize the workplace had failed. Highly repetitive jobs often produced boredom and alienation in the workplace. This criticism became a rallying point for union organization solidarity. Behavioral theorists stepped in to argue that increased production would result if personal goals of employees were coordinated with organizational goals.

Elton Mayo (1880-1949) of Harvard is the father of the human relations theory of management. He led a series of pioneering studies at the Hawthrne plant of the Western Electric Company during 1927 and 1932. In one experiment, workers were given rest periods and productivity increased. When the rest periods were eliminated, productivity again increased. The essence of the now-famous "Hawthorne effect" is that productivity increased because the workers were given special attention. Consequently management should be sensitive to employee needs.

During the early 1950s, the psychologist Abraham Maslow (1908-70 published his now-famous "hierarchy of needs":

1. Basic physiological needs: food, clothing, shelter.
2. Safety and security needs: security from physical or psychological harm.
3. Societal needs: love and friendship.
4. Esteem and status needs: recognition and respect.
5. Self-actualization needs: fulfilling one's potential.

Essentially, he concluded that management can do a lot to human needs and thereby increase productivity.

Since these studies and theories were published, many more have been advanced. Over the years, numerous ideas on management have been forgotten or have been considered temporary fads. Others have stood the test of time, have proved to be useful, and have taken a place in the literature and in the workplace, as we will see in subsequent chapters.

How Can One Become a Successful Manager?

The modern manager requires a whole package of interpersonal and technical skills. Many descriptions of the successful manager have been provided over the years. The necessary qualities include initiative, intellect, perception, foresight, flexibility, and persuasiveness. But how does one acquire the skills to become a successful manager? Many believe that the answer formal education; others see experience as the route to success. The best avenue is an integration of theories and practices that complement each other. Theories are at the foundation of many strategies applied in world. And theories help us comprehend, utilize, and evaluate p experience.

13

Planning and Budgeting

Business Planning

A pharmaceutical firm that invests heavily in research and development would require protection of proprietary information. A retail chain that plans to reduce the number of salespeople per store and rely on customer self-service may have an increase in shop-lifting. The following discussion provides a foundation for basic business planning and illustrates its applicability to S&LP.

Planning is the basis upon which other management functions begin. The organizing and controlling functions, for example, carry out the decisions made during planning. Simply put, planning is advance thinking as the basis for doing. It can be reduced to four distinct, yet interrelated, phases:

Phase 1: Establishing objectives and their priority.

Phase 2: Forecasting future events that can affect the accomplishment of objectives.

Phase 3: Implementing the plans operationally through budgeting.

Phase 4: Stating and implementing policies that direct activities toward the desired objectives.[1]

Planning can be categorized according to time horizons. Numerous factors affect these time horizons, such as the length of time required to recover capital funds invested in plant and equipment. If a corporation buys $10 million worth of new machinery, it should have a plan showing how and when this money will be recovered. Competitiveness is another factor. The greater the competitiveness, the more important short-and intermediate-range plans become as a business responds to changing events. And in fiercely competitive industries, these plans become the life blood of a business, necessitating a sound information security program for survival.

Plans are also categorized according to missions, objectives, strategies, policies, procedures, rules, programs, and budgets. The mission of an organization is its underlying aim, often stated in product or market terms. Mission statements are broad-based and set a foundation for planning. For example, an oil company would have a basic mission of meeting the energy needs of the population. A contract security service company would have a mission of providing protection to clients.

Objectives flow from mission statements but are much more specific. Typical business objectives are profitability, growth, and market share. A security objective would be to reduce internal theft. Strategies establish a program of action to reach objectives. An example would be a specific marketing strategy to sell a new product.

Policies provide direction for thinking and action so that decisions conform to objectives. They are management tools for controlling people. Policies should be clearly written and should be communicated frequently to employees. Procedures delineate a list of steps for employees to follow. In contrast to policies, procedures limit discretion. Procedures assist in fulfilling the requirements of policies. A rule is an inflexible plan that requires specific, definite action for example, "Only authorized personnel beyond this point."

A program is a mixture of objectives, policies, procedures, rules, resources, job assignments, and other elements required to transform a plan into action. A manufacturing company that plans to replace half its equipment within two years would have programs involving finance, training, and maintenance. An S&LP department might have programs that emphasize internal theft counter-measures or rape prevention. A budget is an important management tool that is used to plan and control income and expenditures. In many organizations, it is the primary planning instrument guiding future actions.

Strategic Business Planning

Strategic business planning can be defined as the process of determining how to pursue long-term goals with the resources that are expected to be available. As organizations grow and devote more time to planning greater emphasis is placed on anticipating the future. Changes in the external environment and valves to respond become a major focus of attention. Strategic planning attempts to manage resources to create a competitive edge. To think strategically means to make sense out of an uncertain future he visualizing the interdependency of key factors. This is done through a study of world affairs and technological trends to spot important inter-dependencies. A prime question is how the organization should react to emerging opportunities and obstacles. In our information and technology age, and with diminishing resources, strategic planning becomes vital.

Organizations in the advanced stage of strategic planning actually seek to create and control the future; creativity, wealth, and power are major prerequisites for reaching such goals. Strategic planning is primarily a top management responsibility. However, managers at all levels should be cognizant of this process because of its impact on virtually everything they do.

Planning for Security and Loss Prevention

Planning is a primary management function that results in a design used for reaching objectives. It prepares for change and copes with uncertainty.

Unimpressive planners adhere to the philosophy "We'll cross that bridge when we get to it." In the S&LP field especially, such an attitude can be disastrous. When a serious incident does occur, and there has been no preparation, a "panic atmosphere" will confront an organization and those whose duty it is to prepare and plan. Since "heads will roll," even the most diehard antiplarmers should look at planning as insurance to prevent job loss.

Many executives approach formal planning in a positive manner but procrastinate until they get "some free time." Unfortunately, planning may take place haphazardly, even though good planning can solve many problems. The executive should periodically step out of a busy schedule by setting aside some time for formal planning. Although it takes time to collect data, meet with others, delegate assignments, and develop ideas, once an organized planning process begins, this job becomes easier.

Guidelines for the Planning Process

The following guidelines can help the S&LP executive during the planning process:

— Planning must be An ongoing process, reflecting changing conditions. The ~planner must have a broad view of what is occurring-in the world. This includes economic, political, and social factors that have an impact on business.

— Corporate goals must be reflected in S&LP plans. What do your superior and your superior's superior expect from S&LP? The importance of this question cannot be overstated.

— Those participating in and receiving S&LP services should be part of the planning process. Planning computer security without DP personnel would bea basic blunder.

— Planning should be interdisciplinary. Many fields of study provide answers to protection problems. Marketing strategies, for example, are applicable to S&LP planning.

— Plans for S&LP must be summarized in financial terms. How much will it cost? Are the plans cost-effective? What are the less expensive alternatives? Is there a return on investment?

— Be well prepared for those who cast doubt on your plans. Practitioners can be devastated and discredited if they present protection plans without sound justification.

Decision Making

The following list can be considered a beginning point for developing personalized problem-solving and decision-making strategies.

— Decision making should follow seven steps: (1) stating the problem, (2) gathering relevant information, (3) analyzing information, (4) listing possible solutions, (5) selecting a solution, (6) implementation, and (7) evaluation.

— Thoroughly examine the positive and negative consequences of alternative courses of action.

— Know the costs and risks of negative consequences.

— Give special attention to contingency plans in case unfortunate events occur.

— Through careful planning, reduce the number of decisions that must be made under crisis conditions.

— Be perceptive to personal biases and other personality factors that influence decisions.

— There is considerable evidence that group decision making is superior to individual decision making. An individual often lacks some of the information or skills to arrive at the best possible decision. The more people who work on a problem, the greater the likelihood that someone will devise a viable solution.

— Group decision makes not always practical. During emergency situations, there is no time for participatory management.

— Decisions should be made at the lowest appropriate level. If the enough information or authority to be effective.

— "Flip-flopping" on decisions can be reduced by waiting until sufficient information is available before a decision is made. This is a tricky process, because the key is to figure when appropriate information has been received and when to make the decision.

— Solutions to certain problems lie within existing policies; efforts should not be wasted on devising an original solution unless clear benefits are foreseen.

— Never assume that a problem is solved after a decision has been made. Evaluation and follow-up are vital.

— Consider quantitative methods to analyze alternative solutions to problems. Enlist the aid of a specialist.
— Consider decision trees, which are graphical models, resembling flowcharts, that depict a sequence of choices and possible outcomes. Such decision aids enable an executive to look at and understand a problem that involves a sequence of related events.
— The Delphi forecasting technique uses a panel of experts who, anonymously, make predictions and support their views without meeting face to face. Each expert is informed about the others' views and re-thinks his or her position. Anonymity reduces defensive behaviour and ego problems. The Delphi technique is feasible when decisions do not have to be made quickly.
— To develop new ideas, break away from strictly security sources of information and read outside the field. There are hundreds of trade magazines and journals that contain ideas for security. Business, psychology, sociology, and social psychology are among several disciplines that provide practical information for our field.

Creativity

Because the S&LP executive is faced with an increasingly complex world, many difficult questions surface, and high-quality answers are not always plentiful. One path to problem solving is to unblock the individual's creativity.

As a young person grows up, parents, teachers, and peers can play a role in blocking individual creativity. Socialization and social pressure force people to abandon many of their own unique ideas in favour of social expectations and consensus. When we reach adulthood, we are, in a sense, programmed to think the way we do.'

Creativity and problem-solving capabilities can be stifled unless the individual can break out of this mold and structure the thinking process. Two paths to this end are brain-storming and synectics.

Brainstorming

Brainstorming—a widely used method of producing creative ideas—was developed by Alex Osborn in his book, Applied Imagination. 3 There are four basic rules for brainstorming: (1) no evaluations or criticism as ideas are being developed; (2) the wilder the ideas, the better; (3) the more ideas, the better; and (4) combining, and improving other ideas is welcomed. Brainstorming can be done in a group or by an individual. After all ideas are written down, evaluations begin.

Synectics

The creative process known as synectics, used primarily for technical problems, was developed by William J. Gordon.' Whereas brainstorming promotes a flood of ideas, synectics uses analogies to develop ideas. Blind habit is avoided while problems are perceived in new ways. One excellent example for security purposes would be to study how various animals protect themselves, their families, and their turf from enemies. Another avenue is for the individual to imagine being some element of the problem. If you were a fence, how would you defend yourself against an intruder? What would you design or request to perform a better defensive job?

Management by Objectives

Management by objectives (MBO) has so many variations that it is difficult to describe and evaluate. However, the major focus of MBO is the shift of management from supervision of activities to observation of results. Common elements of MBO are described in the following definition:

> A managerial process whereby organizational purposes are diagnosed and met by joining superiors and subordinates in the pursuit of mutually agreed upon goals and objectives, which are specific, measurable, time bounded. and joined to an action plan; progress and goal attainment are measured and monitored in appraisal sessions which center on mutually determined objective standards of performance.

Management by objectives can be perceived as a management planning tool whereby all employees state objectives to be reached during the year in the course of their work. Participation by all employees, from president to line personnel, is a key ingredient for a successful MBO program. Management by objectives calls for a give-and-take negotiation of objectives between superior and subordinate. Advocates recommend face-to-face meetings between superior and subordinate at least every three months. This allows a check on objectives to see whether they are still valid. Unexpected events may require changes in objectives.

One chief benefit of the MBO process is that it enables employees to obtain a frame of reference regarding what is expected of them. This leads to positive reinforcement (i.e., rewards) from superiors, which increases motivation. Inappropriate behaviour can be corrected through punishment or additional training.

Another practical aspect of the MBO process is performance appraisal, which should emphasize results, not personalities or excuses. When appraising performance, the following behavioral principles should be kept in mind, as motivation increases when:

— participation in decision making and objective setting increases;

— employees know where they stand;
— the pursuit of organizational objectives is accompanied by the achievement of personal objectives;
— employees are recognized for their contributions.

Management by objectives, applied to a loss prevention program would involve a five-step process:

1. Recognition of business and loss prevention needs
2. Establishment of long-term goals
3. Establishment of short-term objectives
4. Implementation of programs
5. Evaluation

Basic business and loss prevention needs point to the prevention and reduction of losses. Specific needs may involve information or executive protection. Goals are long-term accomplishments-for example, reduction of crime losses by 50 percent over three years-where-as objectives are short-term accomplishments, usually for one year. The following are sample S&LP objectives for a retail corporation that is aiming toward increased profitability and greater efficiency from its protection program:

— MBO for S&LP department:

The S&LP department will use available resources and implement strategies to reduce inventory shrinkage by 2 percent within one year.

The S&LP department will use available resources and implement strategies to reduce fraud losses by 25 percent within one year

— MBO for S&LP personnel:

> During the present fiscal year, the corporate S&LP manager will attend a specialized training program on retail inventory shrinkage.
>
> During the present fiscal year, the corporate investigator will attend a training program on retail fraud or study another retailer's countermeasures.

Care must be exercised when formulating an MBO program and objectives. What looks good on paper may be impossible to accomplish. An objective of reducing shrinkage by 5 percent in one year, when it presently stands at 6 percent, could lead to frustration and stress.

The fourth step, implementation, is aided by a host of management tools: policies, procedures, budgets, controls, and so forth.

The fifth step, evaluation, has been neglected over the years. It is very important to find out which programs and strategies are successful and which are not and to pinpoint modifications that can improve existing programs.

Management by objectives does have its-detractors, who claim that a gap exists between theory and practice: "Today, MBO is being used as an exploitive, manipulative management control mechanism as often as a liberating, humanistic philosophy of management. It seems to be venerated more by its abuse than for its proper use."[7]

Despite such criticism, however, MBO enjoys considerable popularity and success in numerous organizations. It is democratic in operation, makes achievement easy to recognize, helps to improve coordination and direction, aids in setting priorities, and is practical. The MBO process puts the practitioner in a more comfortable position when top management asks:

What is security doing to assist corporate objectives? How are the results being measured?

Risk Analysis

Much has been written about risk analysis. Confusion has developed over the years concerning the term itself and whether a formalized risk analysis is really necessary and cost-effective. Here, we will begin our discussion with the basics and then proceed to the problems associated with this management planning tool.

First, let us look at the term risk analysis and define it. As in many fields of study, although several experts may be speaking about the same subject, each may call it by a different name. To simplify our discussion, we will avoid the terms risk assessment and risk evaluation and settle on risk analysis.

Risk analysis can be defined as a management planning tool used to estimate the expected annual loss from specific threats. Risks are a fact of life for businesses, but the degree of risk must be determined before an S&LP program is planned. Basically, this tool allows us to analyze business activities, determine vulnerabilities, study various countermeasures and relevant variables, and make cost-effective recommendations. It is important to remember that the styles of risk analysis and how they are used vary widely.

The following are the steps that should be followed in risk analysis

1. Identify vulnerabilities by performing a comprehensive survey or audit. This entails a thorough study of the organization, its defenses against loss, and its policies and procedures. Key questions relate to the present status, condition, and weaknesses of the S&LP program. An outside

consultant, independent of any security products or services, is a wise choice for providing an objective evaluation. By using different consultants over the years, the organization is likely to obtain interesting and useful perspectives on its program.

The S&LP literature contains many survey or audit checklists. A self-styled survey may be more appropriate for certain industries and organizations. Examples of concerns are physical security, computer and information protection, accounting controls, fire protection, safety, and policies and procedures. A department-by-department evaluation can be conducted.

2. Determine the probability of loss events. Precise mathematical equations delineating the probability of loss events for security have yet to be developed and applied among various industries. Consequently, the practitioner must estimate probabilities subjectively by using such information as industry characteristics, loss history, and available countermeasures. Examples of relevant questions are: What is the probability of a ten-ton steel beam being stolen by an employee? What is the probability of shop-lifting occurring at a large downtown department store in a major urban setting?

3. Figure criticality costs—the dollar costs of serious loss events all they occur. It is imperative that total costs—direct and indirect—be calculated, including death and injury, loss of assets, reduced productivity, extra personnel requirements, presentday replacement costs, and insurance premium hikes. What is the true cost of the robbery and murder of an employee at a fastfood restaurant? Upper management will be more responsive to the true cost of a loss event if it is spelled out in financial terms.

Serious loss events must be prioritized and supported by cost-effective countermeasures. What would have a higher priority—preventing vandalism in a company cafeteria or safeguarding accounts receivable data? Would it be cost-effective to spend $1,500 to protect a petty cash fund of $50?

Quantitative Risk Analysis

Quantitative risk analysis is a detailed process whereby vulnerabilities are quantified and cost-effective measures are eventually determined. Elaborate analyses of well-established protection programs, especially where data processing security is vital, are favoured by many experts. However these analyses can be timeconsuming and costly. The involvement and cooperation of all departments are important. And management support is essential, especially for funding.

Risk analysis involves considerable subjectivity. Decisions have to be made regarding how much time and effort are going to be expended to study risk, which is the most appropriate risk analysis technique, and what will be done with the results. And the basic steps of risk analysis require decisions on vulnerability, probability, and criticality. Values and other estimates are often based on imperfect data, and assumptions may not be valid." Risk analysis should be looked upon as one of several aids to planning.

A single individual doing risk analyses may develop a narrow focus of vulnerabilities and how to deal with them. This often manifests itself in old risk survey checklists that have marginal value. Because so many factors can change an organization and its risks, risk analysis methods must be updated constantly to reflect changes.

A security manager should develop cooperative efforts with, for example, those in risk management, engineering, and emergency planning.'. In this way, many perspectives and sources of information become available. Risk managers often use a management information system (MIS) and financial statements to plan better for risks. Engineers utilize their expertise to fully delineate the consequences of natural or man-made disasters. An emergency planner is more aware of hazards and potentially dangerous situation than other specialists.

Those who perform risk analyses must realize that risk is "in the eyes of the beholder." A former Secret Service agent, a fire marshal, and a security specialist will view risks differently. Each possesses a different background, which surfaces during a risk analysis. Each sees a personal "reality." To counter narrow views of risk, one must become the observer of all observes. This is accomplished through a broad-based interdisciplinary approach study and apply many disciplines. The focus of this book is geared to this need.

Another way to strengthen risk analysis is to make decisions based on facts instead of immediate reactions, common sense, and opinions. This is not easy, but the more decisions are based on facts, the better the plans.

The reader is cautioned against totally ignoring quantitative risk analysis. It is recommended that certain security techniques-such as an encryption decision-be candidates for quantitative risk analysis. But for simpler, widely recognized threats, less sophisticated planning and analysis methods are more cost-effective. Baseline security controls are an example.

Risk analyses and security surveys are frequently conducted annually. This leaves a gap during the year in which threats, hazards, and deviations from established controls may go unnoticed. Operational audits and programmed supervision can fill this void."' The operational audit is a methodical examination or audit of operations (1) to find deviations from established practices, (2) to find loop-holes in controls, and (3) to consider means of improvement. Operational audits are supported by programmed supervision, which means that a supervisor goes through a series of inspections to ensure that the controls for which he or she is responsible are being carried out. The supervisor regularly reports on physical conditions and subordinate conformity to procedures.

Quantitative Aids

Quantitative aids provide input for the executive to make a more informed decision. Experienced practitioners often lack an understanding of these tools and the theories behind them. Frequently, a younger practitioner who has recently completed college studies has these techniques fresh in his or her mind. Superiors should learn from the younger practitioner, just as the neophyte should see the value of experience. Some security personnel find this difficult to do because of resentment, distrust, or ego problems. They continue to rely solely on experience and intuition, even though quantitative aids can be looked upon as an additional source to improve decision-making. For practitioners with no background in this area, one approach is to enroll in basic college-level math and statistics courses, which provide a foundation for quantitative methods. Because of a pervasive "math phobia," this subject matter is often seen as an insurmountable obstacle when it is not. Another approach for the busy practitioner is to recruit a mathematician or statistician for consulting work. The key is to guide these specialists to apply their skills to solve S&LP problems!

An excellent book of quantitative methods for security is Security Administration: A Quantitative

Handbook by R. H. Morneau, Jr., and G. E. Morneau (Butterworths, 1982). Sixty-six problems and solutions on practical topics are highlighted in the work, including graphing to show the effectiveness of security and calculating probabilities to improve the chances for convictions.

Contingency Planning

When contingency plans are available, a "panic atmosphere" is less likely, and organizational survival is enhanced. The following list provides a beginning point for contingency planning:

— Assign responsibility after obtaining management support

— Determine loss events that require contingency plans.

— Include all major areas of an organization in planning.

— Estimate the cost of each loss event.

— Compile early warning signals.

— Prepare complete contingency plans. Consider fires, accidents, natural disasters, and strikes.

— Train for first aid, rescue, and evacuation.

— Communicate and cooperate with public service agencies.

— Plan for the protection and safety of people.

— Protect vital records and valuable assets.

— Plan for recovery of operations. Establish mutual aid pacts.

— Plan for possible disaster at businesses that supply critical products services.

— Ensure that contingency plans are reviewed by

several internal specialists: risk manager, auditor, safety coordinator, and the like.

— Practice and test plans.

— So that contingency plans do not become stale and forgotten, review and revise them several times each year. This ensures that the plans serve organizational needs and are cost-effective.

Types of Budgets

There are numerous types of budgets. Some have been in existence for many years, and others are modifications of older, concepts. The more common types are summarized here.

The line-item or object-of-expenditure budget is the oldest and simplest type of budget. It is easy to construct, since each item and expenses in listed line by line, and it is easy to understand. Two disadvantages are that long-range planning is neglected and it is difficult to ascertain the percentage of the budget devoted to specific loss prevention strategies.

The term program or results budget has been used to describe a variety of practices that have evolved from a mixture of other types of budgets. Essentially, it refers to expenses for specific programs or activities. Such a budget emphasizes a program structure, with identification of the objectives to be achieved. A line-item component is used for fiscal control. An executive will estimate the costs of providing crime prevention services, for example, for a specific per time. A major advantage of this type of budget is that organizational behaviour is directed at specific objectives. It provides a broad basis for justifying and explaining the budget.

The zero-based budget (ZBB) was developed by Peter A. Pyhrr and a team of researchers at Texas Instruments during the late 1960s. Jimmy Carter, when he was governor of Georgia, learned of the technique and it to Georgia and eventually to the federal government as president Aft the ZHB exist other types of budget, it is an innovation designed to improve budgeting, but it has been subjected to considerable controversy. The ZBB aims at preparing a budget without any reference to what was done before. Executives must justify budget cost as if they were being requested for the first time. This is especially useful because be at the end of a budget year, many managers rush to spend all their funds out of fear that next year's budget will be reduced; Furthermore, programs continue to be funded long after positive results have ceased. Incremental budgeting has been blamed for this problem, as past levels of expenditures are automatically assumed to be valid and only newer expenditures requires justification. This process hides wasteful spending and obsolete programs. Questions of consideration that are applicable to S&LP are: Why do specific loss prevention programs and strategies exist? What would happen if each was eliminated? Advantages of the ZBB include the following: budget justification is improved, emphasis can be given to priority programs, marginally effective or nonproductive programs can be rationally eliminated, duplication of effort is reduced, improved information aids planning, and evaluation is strengthened. The chief disadvantages are the time, effort, and resources needed to prepare a ZBB. This is especially so for decision packages, a primary component of ZBB, whereby an executive formulates alternative actions and budgets for each major activity while analyzing costs, purpose, and consequences. Decision packages are then ranked according to the benefits derived. Funding decisions are made according to rank Such judgments are often value-based and difficult to quantify, which leads to politicized decisions in both the public and private sectors . Other than these drawbacks, the ZBB is a useful and cost-effective management control technique. It forces a protection program to maintain superior reporting and record-keeping habits.

Although it is important to be aware of the various types of budgets, in practice it may not be easy to clearly differentiate and categorize them. Most organizations use a hybrid of several approaches to fulfill particular needs or financial characteristics. Also, periodically, fads appear in budgeting that are often modifications of older methods.

Regardless of the budgeting approach, three major expense item must be considered. Salary expenses include loss prevention management, supervisors, investigators, officers, and support personnel. Operating expenses include administrative costs, travel, and professional services. Since expenses can both unpredictable and uncontrollable a contingency fund is advisable. Capital improvement costs pertain to equipment or system purchases. The cost is usually high, but resistance can be overcome by prioritizing needs, spreading the cost over two or more years, or leasing.

From a business management perspective, we can classify budgets as follows:

1. Revenue and expense budget
2. Cash budget
3. Capital expenditure budget
4. Balance sheet budget

It is important to note, again, that the terms used to identify budgets and the styles of budgeting are widely diverse. Some companies do not Oven use the term budget, but prefer the term profit planning; and Hewlett-Packard, for example, replaced the word budgeting with targeting.'

The revenue and expense budget, also called the operating budget, provides an overall view of a company's operations. Revenue from the sale of products or services is the prime source of income; thus, the revenue budget is often referred to as the sales budget. All other budgets must be coordinated with this budget, because revenues from sales define the upper limits of expenses and profits. If revenues fall, upper limits of expenses drop and cutbacks are likely.

The cash budget shows the cash availability and cash requirements of a business. The revenue and expense budget provides data for formulating the cash budget. The importance of the cash budget is sometimes neglected by executives, as can be seen when an inadequate cash flow inhibits efficient business operations. For instance, a shortage of cash may restrict increased inventory purchases required during a busy sales season. A shortage of cash to support budgeted expenditures may signal that accounts receivable are excessive. Although sales elate business people, cash typically does not arrive promptly. Too much money tied up in sales has been the demise of many businesses. Consequently, budgeting cash flow to determine the amounts of cash receipts and disbursements helps to assure a liquid position while strengthening business success.

The emphasis of the captial expenditure budget is on large sums of money tied up for long periods of time for facilities, equipment, and other long-term investments. Research and development, massive advertising for a new market, and executive development programs are all long-range investments that require continuing appropriations. Some companies establish a single appropriation budget, which is broad in scope to accommodate several capital expenditures. A major problem with capital expenditure budgets is that it may take several years to realize results. Considerable planning is at the foundation of these budgets.

The balance sheet budget is a forecast, of the expected financial status of all other financial budgets at the end of the budget period, it is a statement of the relationship between asset and liabilitiess at some future point in time. Management uses this budget to check on the accuracy of preparation the degree to which all other budgets have been met. As a control device deviations in budgets can be shown.

Preparing the Budget

Anticipating the future is an integral part of preparing budgets. The experienced practitioner has a reasonable chance of estimating what will occur next year by studying past and present conditions. In retailing, the security executive is familiar with the demands of holiday seasons. In a hospital, the expiration of a different union contract each year can results in an annual strain on the security force. However, in our complex world, anticipating the future is not always easy. Unexpected events are common to the security profession. A case of embezzlement, a terrorist incident or a disaster can overtax a security budget and necessitate increased expenditures.

Although methods of budget preparation vary considerably among organizations, guidelines usually emanate from top management. A key question is: How much will they allocate for security and loss prevention? The answer depends on many factors. Usually, senior management analyzes overall forecasts related to expected annual revenue and determine how much can be spent on operations. Then a limit is established for all departments in an organization. From the lower levels of the organization each department prepares a budget and forwards it to its respective superior. As budgets rise up the hierarchy, senior management reconciles requests with available funds.

Most managers ask for more than they will probably obtain and hope to receive a great portion of their request. Some departments really do have pressing problems that require considerable funds. Senior management, realizing that emergencies do arise, often holds back money in a contingency fund.

A preliminary budget with supporting justification can assist senior management in decision making and can aid the security executive in formulating an acceptable budget. Reference to organizational and loss prevention objectives is an integral part of the early budget preparation process, to provide direction. The more favourable senior management is toward S&LP objectives, the greater the chance for budget approval. Preliminary budgets typically require modifications and, frequently, a reduction or increase in expenditures.

Whenever feasible, subordinates should have input into the budget preparation process. This participatory management approach supports the basic human relations tenet that people fall their own ideas best.

Managers often prepare a budget by simply using last year's budget. If the world remained tranquil and if twenty years of security experience Meant one year twenty times, such budget preparation would probably be more acceptable. However, twenty years of security work usually equals twenty different years of successes, surprises, and failures, resulting from changing vulnerabilities, laws, technology, and socioeconomic conditions. Thus, the executive should plan and budget for constantly changing conditions.

Using Computers

Computers allow the executive to explore many avenues

in the budgeting process while increasing efficiency and effectiveness. Computer capabilities include spread-sheets, projections of spending, instant updating, and graphs. Various comparisons can be made of each account to the entire budget or of earlier budgets to the present one. A word processor and printer are an immense aid in putting together a budget package after decisions have been made on amounts, justifications, and other relevant information. The technology avoids the work of having to retype the whole budget whenever a change is made.

After a budget is approved, a data base management system (DBMS) can be used to track each expenditure by deducting the appropriate amount and providing periodic reports of amounts remaining in each account that is, reporting how much was spent, on what date, by whom, and to whom.

Because protection programs are constantly facing changing conditions, spread-sheets have tremendous advantages over manual systems. For example, if a new vulnerability surfaces, or corporate profits plummet, a spreadsheet permits a quick, clear view of security strategies and projects that are added, deleted, or modified. A computer can rapidly show the impact of a 5 percent budget cut on all accounts. "What if " scenarios can also aid the executive by providing valuable information in the form of a spreadsheet, graph, or the like.

Return on Investment

An ROI is something that many practitioners may not be accustomed to dealing with in their work. However, if, during difficult economic times, a senior executive who doesn't even know the basics of security tells the security manager that the security budget will be cut unless an ROI can be shown, how will the manager respond? The following information does not offer miraculous answers to solve all ROI problems. Rather, this discussion should be considered a beginning point for increased understanding and a stimulus for creativity.

One popular way to show security as a profit center is to illustrate that an investment in security will lower shrinkage and will have a positive effect on profits. Shrinkage is the percentage of inventory that disappears because of internal theft, shop-lifting, damage, or paperwork errors. Suppose that a company has a sales volume of $100 million and shrinkage at 4 percent, which yields an annual loss of $4 million. Let us say that a $1 million investment in security results in a drop in shrinkage to 1 percent. The expense of $1 million for security thus yields a net savings of $2 million.

Since the shrinkage figure plays a crucial role in judging the effectiveness of security, it is imperative that this figure be accurate. The shrinkage percentage is compiled after a inventory, so a shoddy inventory can distort this figure. In one case an undercover investigator participating in an inventory noticed employees' having difficulty with numbers beyond 999. Something, so basic as plaring commas in large numbers was confusing to employees. Management had assumed that all employees know how to count and record numbers properly, but temporary workers had to be to conduct a more accurate inventory. In another case, a yearly turnover of security staff occurred at a large retail store after annual shrinkage figures were released. The general manager had always blamed shop-lifters and constantly criticized security personnel for not making enough shop-lifting arrests. The operations and security managers were repeatedly asked by an outside consultant to check on how the general manager compiled the shrinkage figure. Specific answers never surfaced, and three group of security personnel departed in three years.

Although a high shrinkage figure may indicate a serious internal or external theft problem, other factors may be influencing shrinkage. Poor records and human error should be considered. In the first case in the preceding paragraph, human error was responsible for an inaccurate inventory. In the second case, the general manager may have been oblivious to multiple factors having a bearing on shrinkage, or he may have been involved in illegal behaviour himself and so blamed others.

Besides the problems associated with shrinkage statistics, a security executive can illustrate ROI by graphically plotting trends in shrinkage for successive years before and after an investment in security.

Another possible avenue to illustrate ROI is through research on loss events. But this is a tricky process. All competent security and loss prevention organizations maintain records of incidents: How many crimes fires, and accidents occur annually? Care must be exercised in designing a quality incident reporting system. When statistics are compiled and interpreted, numerous variables must be must be considered and thoroughly analyzed. For example, if the number of crime events has increased after a major-investment in security, the causative factors should be interpreted with care. Some possible explanations are:

Increased resources permit more security patrols and investigations to expose crimes.

— Employees have been educated regarding which illegal actions should be reported.

— Because employees have more confidence in security, they are reporting more crimes.

— Easier reporting methods are available.

— Prevention strategies have failed, and offenders are finding the corporation a favourable target.

— The crime rate from incident reports may not reflect the actual amount of crime so much as it does the way it which security operates.

The foregoing factors illustrate the complicated nature of analyzing crime statistics. The practitioner must study all variables and must be prepared for myriad questions from senior management.

Research is one way to develop a clearer understanding of crime incidents. Reported crime can be compared to actual victimization. This type of research has been done with the general population to compare crimes reported to the police with actual citizen victimization. Because of factors such as non-reporting, the number of crimes has been shown to be several times higher than what was recorded in official, statistics. The Uniform Crime Reports published by the FBI are notoriously inaccurate, because these statistics are compiled from reported crimes. Although a new or expanded security budget may be followed by an upsurge in reported crime, the situation is likely to stabilize. A downward trend may occur as more and more employee-offenders are purged from the organization and as security obstacles become formidable for outsides. If a point is reached at which the number of crimes decreases substantially, should the protection budget be reduced? No. This is the time when greater attention can be focused on more positive aspects of security and loss prevention, such as prevention strategies and education.

Justifying and Selling the Budget

Budget justification answers the question of why security and loss prevention programs and monies are being requested. The practitioner must be well prepared with supporting research and documentation to substantiate each item in the budget and how it will deal with potential losses.

When the S&LP budget is reviewed by senior management officials, they may ask any of the following questions:

— What is the total cost of the security and loss prevention program?

— Does S&LP fit into the mission and goals of our organization? How?

— What percentage of the budget is allocated to each major strategy?

— Is each strategy cost-effective? How?

— Are there less expensive ways to reach S&LP objectives? What about placing more emphasis on contracting security?

— Are the strategies practical?

— Are the strategies really needed?

— What are similar industries doing?

— Will the strategies interfere with productivity?

— How will employees and customers react to this program?

— Has participatory management been used to prepare these plans and budget?

— Do our potection people have the training to do the job?

— Have all applicable laws been checked?

— Is there any chance of increased liability?

— Can we obtain any reductions on insurance premiums?
— How will you evaluate these strategies for effectiveness?
— Can any older strategies be eliminated to save money?
— What kinds of results can we expect from the program?
— Will there be an ROI?

Because the budgetary process is so important as a foundation for protection efforts, the practitioner should always be looking to sharpen his or her budgeting skills by acquiring new and better ideas. The following points are presented for this purpose.

—A continuous dialogue between the protection executive and senior management, starting from the early stages of the planning and budgeting process, will assist the practitioner in preparing sound budget justification according to the guidelines and needs of senior management.
— It is vital to understand the personalities and background of senior management and the business goals they represent.
— Expert salespeople work at finding out what their customers needs and problems are; then they recommend good solutions. You are selling your ideas; try to convince the senior executives that your ideas will help them and the company.
— Think like a business person specializing in S&LP. Present the program in financial terms.
— Remember, businesses exist to make money, not arrests.

— Strive to be flexible and open-minded, especially to business concepts. Illustrate the true costs of loss incidents. Direct losses are obvious, such as the cost of a machine stolen from a plant. Indirect losses are typically hidden: replacement cost at today's price, lost production, temporary substitute costs, cost for investigation and support personnel, and insurance premium hikes.

— Consider charging departments in a company for security services rendered and maintaining accurate records of the costs for security for each department. Such information illustrates how much money is needed for each department for subsequent budgets.

— Justify the budget through loss trends illustrated by shrinkage statistics and summaries of incident reports. Compile industrywide figures for comparison.

— Exercise care when presenting statistics. Senior executives are usually aware of the ways in which statistics can be manipulated.

— Use records to show the value of protection-for example, system reports that list the number of times attempts were made to access secure areas or data, or a log of the number of times supplemental power is supplied, to show the value of backup generators.

— Emphasize that S&LP efforts prevent litigation. Use court cases and cite civil awards. Also point out liability insurance coverage limit and high premiums.

— Compile a list of accomplishments of personnel-for example, that Officer Joe Brown saved a multi-million-dollar inventory by turning off the sprinkler system and extinguishing a small fire by himself, or that an internal investigation prevented the loss of valuable proprietary information. Illustrations that can be expressed in monetary terms will impress senior management.

— Present reports of on-site inspections and surveys by police and fire departments, OSHA, and other government agencies. Safety and protection deficiencies exposed in this manner may have a significant impact on management.

— Use outside consultant recommendations.

— Prepare protection impact statements for pending business expansion or operations involving more serious threats.

— Ensure that the budget is completely understood before it is presented to superiors. Obtain answers to questions by conducting research and contacting peers who may be familiar with your type of situation.

— Be prepared with counter-arguments to anything presented, but exercise diplomacy.

— Unfortunately, a serious incident often, motivates management to look closer at security for answers. If this occurs, be prepared with a comprehensive plan and budget.

— Planning and budgeting are functions that should be thought through about the year. Early preparation and a constant generation of ideas will ultimately improve the protection program.

Quantitative Methods

In an earlier discussion, we noted the difficulty of interpreting corporate or public crime statistics. Since the protection executive frequently prepares reports and presentations to senior management based on known crimes, the unreported incidents should also be a part of the information superiors. Probabilities can play a role in bringing to the surface the true extent of crimes and other incidents.

Budget Presentation

The latter part of the budget process commonly involves some type of presentation. This can be anything from a simple written request to a fully documented proposal backed up by slides, charts, and graphs. The corporate culture dictates what is required. Presentations can take hundreds of hours to prepare. Top executives may be interested in lengthy explanations and may ask numerous questions. On the other hand, an S&LP executive who invested many hours of hard work in preparing to "sell" the security budget may be told: "You only have ten minutes, so make it quick." If the S&LP executive is unsure of what to expect at a budget meeting, he or she must be fully prepared for all possibilities.

Curbing Budget Cuts

Sound budget justification can lead to a budget increase. However, this positive result of hard work and effort is often not the case. Many budgets remain at the same level of funding as earlier years, despite negative factors such as inflation and newer vulnerabilities. And worse than a budget that remains the same is a budget cut.

Imaginative solutions are the foundation of countermeasures to financial woes. One way to halt a reduction in funding is for the protection to broaden his or her skills in fields such as risk management, personnel administration, building management, communication system, and fleet management. When austerity strikes, the practitioner may want to take on more duties to make him or herself more valuable if it means that the protection program can be saved. This runs counter to specializing in security, but the more specialized the individual, the less flexibility is available for difficult budget decisions. On the other hand, there is a limit to the "hats" one can wear and the amount of work that can be delegated. But decisions and sacrifices must be made to enhance the protection program's financial position.

To lessen the impact of ups and downs of the economy, automation can be employed. For example, CCTV and electronic access controls established during good economic times can pay off handsomely if personnel are reduced during a budget cut.

Support for S&LP can possibly be obtained from other departments if they are not also fighting for monies. The risk management and legal departments can be recruited to provide information on the adverse consequences of cutting protection. Litigation after a loss, liabilities, and insurance premium hikes are some of the negative factors prompting the need for full funding for S&LP.

Employee groups can also provide support. If the grapevine spreads the word that fewer security officers will patrol on-premises crime-prone areas employee pressure may become an asset.

Contracting out work formerly done in-house is a growing trend to save money. However, contracting security officers and alarm monitoring and servicing may not be appropriate for all organizations.

Jobs can be combined. If an in-house alarm technician's position is eliminated to contract the work to an outside firm, perhaps the technician can assume other duties in the protection program while assisting with alarm problems.

Above all, ROI must occupy a prominent position in the budget battle. Senior management should be shown that a budget reduction will reduce investment returns.

Index

Accident category, 6
Accident, frequent sources of, 8
Accident records, 31
Acceptable dress code, 51
Accident investigation, 51
Accident reporting, 51
Adequate light, 9

Benefit packages, 51
Business planning, 239

Chemical products, 17
Chair falls, 22
Company safety, 1
Controlling office hazards, 8
Conference method, 44
Cumulative trauma, 6

Disabling accidents, type of, 5
Disability injuries, 5

Equitable life, 4
Employee morale, 9
Employee service, 9
Evaluation uniforms of, 10
Equipment hazards, 11
Electrical code, 12
Effective training programme, 36
Evaluation, methods of, 39
Eye wash, 52
Employee attitude, 88

File drawers, 14
Folding machines, 20
File protection, 25
Fire extinguisher, 26
Fire wash, 52

Good House keeping, 21
Group techniques, 44
Group techniques, 47

Health training, 28
Health committee, 30
Health professionals, 32
Human relations, 41
Housekeeping standards, 51

Inventory clerks, 2
Injury, primary cause of, 3
Industrial accidents, 3
Injury, causes of, 22
Individual techniques, 44
Instruction training, 44
Industrial accidents, 77
Industrial safety, 132

Job performance, 32
Job satisfaction, 41
Job training, 44

Ladder use, 52
Loss prevention, 242

Materials storage, 24
Machine guarding, 51
Maritime workers, 3

Mechanical ventilation, 11
Mechanical safety, 122

Office safety, 1
Office injuries, seriousness of, 2
Office injuries, 2
Office accidents, causes of, 3
Office workers, 7
Office design, 10
Office buildings, 11
Office equipment, 15
Office machines, 18
Office personnel, 23
Office employees, 27

Physiological effect, 9
Purchase chaise, 16
Printing services, 19
Physical space, 37
Personal staffing, 37
Personnel replacements, 37
Programme objectives, 42
Policy statements, 51
Planning and budgetary, 233

Quality desks, 16

Routine safety, 29

Safety professional, 1
Safety programmes, 2
Safety tips, 16
Safety behaviour, 28
Safety training, 32
Safety training needs, 40
Student salaries, 37
Staffing and controlling, 159
Strategic business planning, 241

Train workers, 15
Training, critical aspects of, 29
Training policy, 35
Training budgets, 36
Training materials, 37
Transportation costs, 37
Training, purpose of, 39
Training methods, 43

Visual fatigue, 10

Worker training, 50